Bye-Bye
BOOBS

Bye-Bye BOOBS

My Real Ones Tried To Kill Me
& My Fake Ones Made Me Sick

Holly K. Thrasher

Sweet Blossom Press

First edition paperback original published 2020
Sweet Blossom Press, Palm Desert, CA

This publication contains the opinions and ideas of its author. It is intended to provide helpful and informative material on the subjects addressed in the publication. It is sold with the understanding that the authors and publisher are not engaged in rendering medical, health, or any other kind of personal professional services in the book. The reader should consult his or her medical, health, or other competent professional before adopting any of the suggestions in this book or drawing inferences from it. The authors and publisher specifically disclaim all responsibility for any liability, loss, or risk, personal or otherwise which is incurred as a consequence, directly or indirectly, of the use and application of any of the contents of this book.

Photographs by Ashleigh Taylor Henning (Ashleigh Taylor Portrait)
Photographs by Wiley D. Thrasher
Interior and cover design by Holly K. Thrasher
Copy Editing by Vance K. Thrasher

Library of Congress Control Number: 2020902104

ISBN 978-1-7326172-2-3

For Wiley and Vance

Contents

Introduction

Bye-Bye Boobs is the second unplanned book in my life. When I published *Bittersweet: A Vulnerable Photographic Breast Cancer Journey* in 2018, I was pretty sure that the cherry blossom tattoos that covered my completed breast reconstruction would be the final chapter in my story. Nope! Life threw me a curve ball, well actually, flattened me out!

Not long after *Bittersweet* made its debut and I started my promotional book tour, I was sidelined by debilitating exhaustion, shortness of breath, breast pain, and dozens of other unexplained symptoms. The perfect people were placed in my life to provide me the missing links to discover the cause of my symptoms. My beautiful reconstructed breasts were making me very sick. I had never heard of breast implant illness but once I discovered it, it could not be denied.

I feel that my experience with breast cancer and now breast implant illness needs to be shared. I was caught completely off-guard by the symptoms and cure. I feel betrayed by the implant manufacturers, the FDA (Federal Drug Administration), my original plastic surgeon, and all of the people that should have protected me from this illness. At the very minimum I should have been warned about the possibility of symptoms and complications so I would know what to look for if they occurred. The research is there, but the information has continually been minimized and hidden, and in a lot of cases never shared with patients.

We are not given the list of implant ingredients or even warned of the potential for autoimmune issues, cancer, and even death. I hope this book helps get the word out to those that need it and provides the information to help make informed decisions. If you want breast implants you need to know all of the risks before you make that choice. If you already have breast implants you need the same information, so if you start to have problems you will know if, when, and how to safely explant.

I have come full circle from having breasts to no breasts, then reconstructed with breast implants, and then choosing to return to totally flat with no breasts. It has been a wild ride and had I known what I know now, I would never have put silicone breast implants in my chest cavity endangering my health and life.

This book is not a substitute for professional medical care. Do not use this book as an alternative to a consultation with your physician. Only a qualified medical professional can evaluate your case and recommend treatment. I have made every effort to make sure that at the time of publication the information is accurate. However, new findings and recommendations may invalidate some of what has been presented. For the most accurate information, always consult your healthcare professionals and only trust those professionals that are well educated about breast implants and the illnesses they cause.

Holly K. Thrasher

Chapter One
Your Boobs Look Amazing

I hadn't felt like myself since I had a set of 525CC, Allergan Natrelle® Silicone Breast Implants tucked under both pectoral muscles after my double mastectomy and breast reconstruction surgeries. In fact, I started losing *me* almost immediately, but I had no idea, because it was so subtle.

I was so thrilled to have big, perky, beautiful breasts again after surviving breast cancer and a double mastectomy, but the breast implants had only been in my body for about two months when I realized that something wasn't right. The first symptom I noticed was my left leg became very stiff and all of my leg muscles and joints began to ache. If I sat for any length of time, when I got up, there would be a shooting pain that traveled mid-thigh down to the ball of my foot. I could barely walk and I hobbled around like a ninety-year old until the stiffness and pain dissipated which took about a minute or two.

It wasn't just the joints and muscles in my legs that seemed inflamed. As time went on, my neck, back, shoulder, arms, and chest also began to hurt. Some days everything ached for no reason.

What in the world is going on? I mentioned it to my oncologist at the time and she told me I probably had neuropathy left over from chemotherapy.

Neuropathy is permanent nerve damage that can be attributed to chemotherapy. That seemed reasonable, the chemo was truly awful and I had been told there could be permanent side effects. My oncologist was the one with the experience and knowledge about these things, so I assumed she must know what she was talking about.

Out of an abundance of caution, I mentioned the new symptoms to my plastic surgeon, my primary care physician, and even my physical therapist. All three of them had different variations of the same reasoning. I had been through breast cancer, undergone a double mastectomy with nipple removal, completed four grueling rounds of chemotherapy, I was in my late forties and now in menopause as a result of the removal of both ovaries and fallopian tubes. Apparently, all good reasons for feeling old and decrepit. *That must be it. What else could it be?*

It would take me over two years to finally figure it out and without the help of any of my doctors. Sometimes it's hard to see something even though it is right in front of you. Literally right in front of me. It didn't help that everyone I trusted to know the answers was telling me that everything was fine, nothing to worry about.

I believe that as women, we are born with a knowing, an innate sense when something seems off, but we don't always listen to ourselves and even if we do listen, sometimes it is impossible to get anyone else to take our concerns seriously. It is easy to turn off that knowing, that gut feeling when we are told otherwise by medical professionals.

I really didn't want anything else to be wrong and I needed to believe that everything was fine, but my gut kept telling me to talk to my doctors, so I did. I mentioned one or more of the symptoms every time I met with them. They never took me seriously and I was dismissed at every turn. *I believe that I am a very strong advocate for myself having been through breast cancer, but clearly, there is always room for improvement.*

Nobody ever told me I was crazy, but there was a lot of silence and shoulder shrugging when I complained to my doctors. I wouldn't be surprised if there was eye rolling and conversations behind my back between physicians and their assistants too.

It was also clear, that when a doctor viewed my reconstructed breasts and gorgeous cherry blossom tattoos, my case for anything being wrong with them got weaker. I was one of the lucky ones. My breast reconstruction was beautiful. Every time a medical professional saw them for the first time, they would ask me who my plastic surgeon was and confirm that he had done a great job reconstructing my chest. The consensus was that my reconstruction was one of the best they had seen.

I had put together a team of doctors that I quite literally trusted with my life when I was originally diagnosed in 2015. My general surgeon had done an amazing job removing both breasts, both nipples, and the cancerous tumor. She artfully left just enough breast tissue surrounding both breast pockets so that when the implants were placed during the reconstruction phase, the results would be very natural.

Once my general surgeon had completed her task, I was handed off to a plastic surgeon that she highly recommended and worked with frequently. The next step would be deciding how the plastic surgeon would reconstruct what I had lost. After my initial consultation with the plastic surgeon, I knew he was the one to do my reconstruction. He was kind, he listened, and he had a stellar reputation among breast cancer survivors.

Looking back, one of the things that was definitely missing in all of my conversations with doctors was the option of going flat and not reconstructing. Nobody ever offered it as a legitimate option. I wasn't given any reading materials that included it. Everyone was pushing reconstruction and encouraging me to replace my breasts. The general thinking was that as a woman I would be far better off with breasts than without. I was 46 years old at the time of diagnosis and that was considered very young to have breast cancer. It was assumed I had a very long life ahead of me and I would be happiest living that life with breasts. It was explained to me that there were various options to accomplish this necessary breast replacement.

I could choose to do a TRAM flap procedure that would use my own muscle, fat, and tissue cut from my abdomen and then flipped up into my chest area to mold new breasts. I remember him telling me there was a high satisfaction rate with this procedure, because they would be part of my own body. My plastic surgeon said the surgery would take about 12 hours for him to complete. I knew immediately that I was not up for that lengthy surgery and the 2-3 months of recovery.

According to a 2018 study, the TRAM flap complication rate has been estimated to be around 46.9% which was considered extremely high compared to the other reconstruction options. The failure rate for TRAM flap was 2.1% [i] Failure meant that either the tissue died, necrosis, or for one reason or another the incisions did not heal properly and the procedure could not be completed. I knew that my abdomen muscles would be permanently damaged and that seemed like it could cause me other issues down the road, so I said "No, thank you!"

The next option offered to me was DIEP flap, a procedure using belly fat. An incision would be made along my bikini line and part of my skin, fat, and blood vessels would be moved up to my chest to make small breast mounds. My plastic surgeon did not think that I had enough fat to make this procedure work. Quite frankly, I wasn't interested in DIEP either as it was a major surgery with a fairly long recovery and all the same possible issues as the TRAM flap.

The rate of complication for DIEP had been estimated at approximately 34% [ii] which was better than TRAM, but still high. Keep in mind, I only know about the complication rates now that I am doing research for this book. These statistics were never shared with me while I was in the decision-making mode. I had no idea at the time that both TRAM and DIEP had pretty significant complication rates and rates of complete failure.

With TRAM and DIEP off the table and no information or consideration for reconstructing to flat given, it was looking like the only viable option I was willing to do was to reconstruct with breast implants.

I was told that reconstructing with breast implants was fairly easy and extremely common for someone in my position to choose. According to the same study I cited above from 2018, breast reconstruction with implants had the smallest complication rate, approximately 24.7%, but the highest failure rate at 5.9%, but I didn't know any of these rates at the time.[iii]

Breast reconstruction with implants was described as the easiest route to regaining breasts after a double mastectomy, so I took it. I do not want to place the full blame on my decision to reconstruct with any of my medical professionals at the time for several reasons. The first being that I was anxious to get my life back on track and with as little change as possible. My breasts were missing, so it made total sense at the time to try to get them back if in fact that was a safe and sane option. Breast implants were presented as not only safe and reliable, but as heavily studied and a proven medical device.

I realize now that I was in a very vulnerable position having to make all of these major decisions while also fearing for my life. The FDA website includes a complete list of possible complications as a result of breast implants which include; breast pain, atrophy of the skin and tissue, capsular contracture, inflammation, irritation, seroma, ALCL lymphoma, connective tissue disease, reproductive problems, systemic problems, breastfeeding issues, effects on children and many more.[iv] I believe that I should have been told about all of the possible complications and long-term issues of living with breast implants.

I also believe that I should have been given information about reconstructing to flat as a viable option. Had I chosen that route, I would most-likely only had one surgery and been done with it. I would not have had to suffer through five different surgeries, anesthesia, and all they entail.

It would have also been helpful to know that I didn't have to make any decisions about reconstruction right away. There is no mandatory time frame for reconstruction. I could have taken a year or two to think about it if that had been presented to me. *The question that plagues me now is "Did I have enough information to make an informed decision about breast reconstruction with implants?"* More on that later.

After choosing reconstruction with implants, my plastic surgeon placed Allergan textured expanders under my pectoral muscles to expand the breast pockets to receive the implants. For almost 3 months, I would go to his office every couple of weeks and he would add saline to the expanders to increase them slowly. This expansion was stretching my skin and tissue, so that I would have enough space for the implants.

What I didn't know at the time was under the muscle implants can only be placed by cutting and dissecting part of the pectoral muscles. When this is done, you can experience chronic pain and weakness in the chest and the arms. Something I was never warned about and didn't find out about until years later when I was actually experiencing it.

After my expanders were filled to capacity, my plastic surgeon then removed the expanders, reconstructed my chest, and placed the implants. The final result was perfectly symmetrical breasts that looked amazing. At the time, I was thrilled with the results and documented the whole experience using photos of every stage in my first book, *Bittersweet*.

After a full year of healing, my tattoo artist, Sebastian Orth of Otherworld Tattoo in Santa Barbara, covered my breast cancer scars with brightly colored cherry blossom tattoos. I was done and my breasts were beautiful. It was quite an impressive team of experts all coming together with what I believed at the time was my best interest at heart and doing what they did best. And yet, four years later I was dealing with the consequences of my doctor's lack of transparency with the real facts as they relate to breast implants. I cannot believe how much I didn't know about breast implants and I had a set in my chest for almost three years.

My intension with *Bittersweet* was to demystify the breast cancer process for everyone to see and to give not only information, but to give hope to those women who would be diagnosed in the future. My original cancer diagnosis in 2015 to final reconstruction and completed tattoos in 2017 took exactly two years to complete. I had survived breast cancer, written a book about it, and I was relieved to have my life back and to share what I had learned with the world.

My first book, *Bittersweet*, is laid out on the following timeline and included vulnerable photos showing the process of transformation of my breasts and life through breast cancer. Each chapter included helpful tips on how to get through each phase comfortably.

Bittersweet Timeline

✿	11/18/15	Diagnosed with stage 2 breast cancer (infiltrating ductal adenocarcinoma)
✿	12/17/15	Total double mastectomy surgery
✿	2/2 to 4/5/16	4 Rounds of chemotherapy
✿	5/18/16	Breast tissue expander surgery
✿	5/18 to 8/2/16	Breast tissue expanded for breast implant placement
✿	7/5/16	No evidence of cancer on first tumor marker test (Cancer is gone!)
✿	8/17/16	Expanders replaced with silicone implants
✿	8/30/17	First tattoo session, 1 year since implants placed
✿	10/10/17	Ovaries and fallopian tubes removed to put me back in menopause
✿	11/12/17	Final tattoo session to complete my breast cancer journey
✿	10/06/18	*Bittersweet* Book Launch

At the time of *Bittersweet*'s publishing, I felt a sense of completion for the end of my breast cancer journey and a sense of a new beginning to my life as a breast cancer survivor. The final chapter of *Bittersweet* showed the gorgeous photos of my completed breast reconstruction and was supposed to be the end of the story. I never imagined that my breast implants would make me sick and that I would have to uncover the hidden truth about breast implants and have them removed to regain my health.

Chapter Two
Something is Wrong with Me

We had lived in Ojai, California for fourteen years and I had transitioned from being the local candy lady to breast cancer survivor. At the time of my diagnosis, I owned and operated Kingston's Candy Co., a nostalgic candy store in the heart of downtown Ojai. The retail store had been open for six years and it was just a little over a year and a half since I had opened Candy Makes Life Sweeter, a wholesale private label candy company based out of the same location. Both businesses had finally begun to make us money and I truly thought that I had found my calling as the candy lady. Sadly, both businesses were victims of my cancer diagnosis and we closed them so I could focus on my treatment.

Living in a small town definitely has its benefits, but one of the drawbacks included not being able to go anywhere without running into someone that I knew. I was constantly reminded of my cancer journey and the loss of the candy store by well-intentioned friends and neighbors. I literally could not go downtown without someone telling me how much they missed the candy store and wanting to know how I was doing or if I would be reopening sometime in the future. I loved them for all of the support, but also felt like I needed a reprieve from it. I was struggling with my personal identity post cancer and needed a major change.

Our son, Vance, was turning eighteen years old and entering his final year of high school. Both Wiley and I started to ask ourselves *"What do we want to do?"* I had survived cancer and lived to see Vance move from childhood into adulthood. It felt like a huge accomplishment and a huge relief.

Wiley and I started to discuss the possibility of a major life change. The more we talked about it, the more excited we became about packing it all up and starting a new adventure in a new, bigger city. Wiley and I were both turning 50 in 2019 and had been married for 25 years. It was time for something new and exciting. We knew we wanted to stay close to family and friends in California and since we already had family living in the California desert, it seemed like the perfect place to start exploring.

After several trips scouting out neighborhoods and houses in the desert, we couldn't shake the idea of starting a whole new chapter in our lives. We told Vance that we would wait for him to graduate from Nordhoff High School in Ojai and then we would move. Vance thought about it for a couple weeks and then told us that we didn't have to wait and we should just go now. We put our house on the market and started to search for the perfect desert house to purchase.

It was the middle of the Summer and the triple digit heat was stifling, but Wiley and I planned a house hunting trip to the desert for the weekend. We saw an open house sign at the entrance to one of the country clubs in Palm Desert and decided to check it out. We had been looking at houses all day and Wiley was over it. After several days house hunting in intense heat, he didn't want to go in this particular open house, because it was clearly too small, not the right style of house, and not in the neighborhood we were looking for. I don't know why, but I insisted that we stop.

Wiley stayed in the car with the air conditioning on and I walked up the driveway in the sizzling sun to check it out. When I entered, a gorgeous blonde dressed in hot pink took one look at me and said, "Are you a breast cancer survivor?' I was a little baffled and wondered how in the world would she know that, "Yes, I am," I proudly told her, "How did you know?" She went on to explain that she didn't know many women that would tattoo their breasts unless they had been through breast cancer. I hadn't realized my cherry blossom breast tattoos were that visible in the dress I was wearing, but it made perfect sense.

Kathleen (Sunshine) O' Brien, was my first new friend in the desert and also a breast cancer survivor. She and her two sisters had breast cancer at the very same time in 2012 and shared their story on The View, The Today Show, and countless other interviews. She was a breast cancer celebrity in the desert and also just a warm, fun, and sunny person. We hugged that day as I left her open house and we became friends on Facebook to keep in touch. More than a year after that fateful meeting, Wiley, Vance, and I were settled into our new desert home and none of us at the time knew how valuable that meeting and my friendship with Sunshine would ultimately be.

The photo of me on the next page hardly looks like me. The photo was taken April 2016 and I was only forty-seven years old and living a nightmare due to my current circumstances. I didn't think I would ever get breast cancer in my forties and doctors kept telling me that statistically that should have been the case. Even with an aggressive cancer diagnosis I was extremely hopeful that I would be able to put this all behind me after all of my surgeries and treatments were complete. I was healing and waiting to start breast reconstruction after my double mastectomy and was bald and covered in hives from chemotherapy. I felt miserable most days and desperately wanted my old life back, but I knew that if I kept pushing forward with reconstruction I would look and feel normal again so I kept smiling for the camera and hoping for the best.

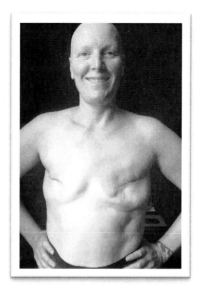

Bald with red itchy hives and still healing from my double mastectomy, April 2016. The extra skin and tissue was left behind to help build a base for breast reconstruction with breast implants

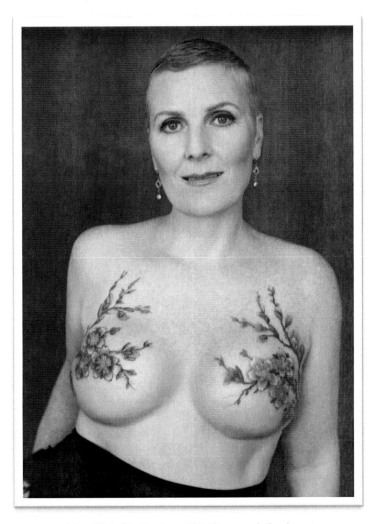

May 2018 - Feeling beautiful after completing breast
reconstruction with implants and cherry blossom tattoos.
Photo by Ashleigh Taylor Portrait

The second photo was taken in May 2018 with professional hair and makeup and the talent of an amazing photographer, Ashleigh Taylor Portrait. The photoshoot was to be the final chapter of *Bittersweet*. I had come along way between these two photos and was nearing what I thought was the end of my journey and the beginning of my long-awaited book tour.

We were new to desert living and I was moving full speed ahead with my book launch and all of the speaking and book signing engagements it would bring. I pushed myself hard, because I needed to get my book out into the world. My book launch party was a dream come true as all of my friends and family joined me back in Ojai to celebrate not only the book, but the end of my cancer nightmare. I booked events at Chaucer's Books in Santa Barbara and several Barnes & Noble bookstores in California. I was so happy to have found my voice and a subject that I was passionate about, so I spoke at several fundraisers and I wanted to do more, but I was hitting a wall.

After a jam-packed October and November promoting *Bittersweet*, I was exhausted. So much so that I couldn't find the energy to book anymore events in 2018. I decided I would take the entire month of December off for the holidays and return to my mission in January of 2019. I assumed this break would leave me well rested and ready to roll in the New Year, but unfortunately that didn't happen.

January rolled right by and I could barely muster the energy to complete my daily chores and activities. I felt wrecked. A long list of symptoms had begun to dictate what I could accomplish every day and more and more things on my to-do list kept getting bumped to the next day or never got completed. I started to feel depressed and hopeless. I started to cry in the shower, something I hadn't done since in the middle of dealing with cancer. I had no idea what was causing this mental and physical decline, but I had to rest when my body told me to. In the moments when I felt better I had to move quickly before I was down again.

I started to notice that when I exercised I felt good that day, but was completely wiped out the next. The same was true for attending events. I could muster the energy needed to attend, but I needed to stay in bed the next day to recover. As a result, I started to limit my activities and decline invitations to do things.

I wasn't just feeling exhausted, I was feeling confused and experiencing memory loss and brain fog. It got so bad that one day while talking on the phone with my cousin, Carolynne, she asked me my address and I had no idea! I couldn't remember the house numbers or the street I lived on. I stood holding the phone in my hand trying to recall where I lived and nothing would present itself. I told her to hang on and I walked out my front door and into my driveway to look at the numbers on my house. I then looked down the block at the street sign and the information was finally restored. I felt panic at the fact that lapses in my memory were occurring more and more frequently. I started to wonder if I had early onset dementia or Alzheimer's. I was freaked out!

It was also hard not to worry that maybe my cancer had returned and was metastasizing through my body causing me to feel weak and sick. I followed up with my oncologist, but all of my tests came back normal including my tumor marker test. *If my cancer wasn't back, what was causing me to feel so bad?*

I did the best that I could every day, but it was exhausting being me. I began to feel angry and resentful about my original cancer diagnosis. I had thought that I had worked through all of my feelings regarding it when writing *Bittersweet*, but this unexplained decline in my health was making me question everything once again.

October 6, 2018 – Holly signing books at her *Bittersweet* book launch party at the Ojai Valley Woman's Club in Ojai, California

October 8, 2018 – Holly speaking at the Ojai Cares fundraiser
event at the Topa Topa Mountain Winery in Ojai, California
Photo by Paul Del Signore

October 9, 2018 – Chaucer's Bookstore in Santa Barbara, California
with family friend, Ronaldo Boutin coming out to support me.
My parents used to take my sisters and I to Chaucer's as kids and
I have such fond memories there. Photo by Alma Boutin

October 19, 2018 – Mercury Lounge in Goleta, California.
Surrounded by friends, this was one of the most fun book signing
events I have done. Photo by Melanie Garst

October 20, 2018 – Holly signing and selling books at a
Barnes & Noble event for local authors in Ventura, California

November 17, 2018 – Holly signing and selling books
at Barnes & Noble in Palm Desert, California

It wasn't just a lack of energy and the feeling of being ill that plagued me. I was also experiencing physical symptoms that were hard to ignore. My dream breasts after surviving breast cancer were beginning to bother me. I was also still experiencing unexplained daily joint and muscle pain. The symptoms were hardly the end of the world compared to what I had already been through, at least that's what I kept telling myself.

When I looked in the mirror it was hard not to be pleased with the final results of several years of pain and anguish. My fake breasts looked amazing. All of the stress and worry I had put my husband, Wiley, and our teenage son, Vance through needed to be behind us. My whole family including my loving mother-in-law,

Karen, and both sisters and their families needed final closure. I believed that I deserved closure too. We all needed for this chapter to be behind us so that we could return to our regularly scheduled lives and I could start to live again for something other than my breasts.

Vance had been hearing about my breasts since his Freshman year in high school and now as a Freshman in college he asked me if we were ever going to stop talking about them. I had to laugh, because I truly wanted that, but I didn't make any promises as I tried to ignore the warning signs my body was currently sending.

After we relocated to the desert, the plan was originally for me to continue promoting my book and to get a job once my engagements were completed. As much as I wanted to, I knew I couldn't pull it off. I was really struggling with my energy and felt sick and wiped out most days. I was convinced by my doctors that menopause was kicking my ass and that all of the symptoms must be the result of all of the crap that I had already been through.

Chapter Three
Discovering BII (Breast Implant Illness)

It was the first week of February 2019 and Wiley and I had just celebrated 25 years of marriage before he left for an annual business trip out of state. Vance was at school and only the cat, Tiger, and I were home. I opened my computer and logged onto Facebook to see what was going on with my friends and family. I noticed that my friend, Sunshine, had recommended I join a Facebook group called *Breast Implant Illness and Healing by Nicole.*

It was an all-woman group with over 50,000 members at the time from all over the world. *My first thought was why did Sunshine join me to this group?* I scrolled down the page and read the very personal stories, some including graphic photos of breasts and implants. I felt a mix of shock and disbelief as I read post after post from women, just like me, that were experiencing debilitating symptoms that were sidelining them from their lives. We all had one thing in common, breast implants.

I spent the entire day glued to my computer screen absorbing everything I read about breast implants, their history, their toxic ingredients, their ability to create an autoimmune response in the body, and the emerging cancer BIA-ALCL (breast implant associated - anaplastic large cell lymphoma) that had killed over a dozen women and infected over 400 as of early 2019.

I cried and couldn't shake the pit in my stomach as I explained to Wiley over the phone what I had discovered that day. Wiley was a thousand miles away in Texas and unable to do much to comfort me as he had work he needed to focus on. I was so upset that I had trouble sleeping that night.

The next day, I wracked my memory for the information that I had known before deciding on implants and all of the new information I had discovered for the first time. *How did I not know about all of this?*

I remembered back to my very first plastic surgery consultation in early 2016. Wiley and I had met with the recommended plastic surgeon to discuss my possible reconstruction and to get information to make decisions about how to move forward. I had come across some information on the internet about a rare cancer associated with implants and I asked about it. The plastic surgeon assured us that the cancer was only caused by textured tear-drop shaped implants and that he did not use that type for that very reason. He only used smooth implants in his patients. I don't even remember if he called it by its name, ALCL. It wasn't anything I would have to worry about, so I never thought about it again until recently.

I also asked if there was anything else that could go wrong with the implants that I should be aware of. He told Wiley and I that breast implants were not lifetime devices and they would need replacing. He recommended replacing them in eight years and no longer than ten years from when they were implanted. He mentioned that ruptures could occur, but were very rare. He said swapping them out was a fairly easy surgery, they would make a small incision to remove the old ones and just insert the new ones. He also mentioned that the newer generation of implants were cohesive, meaning they weren't like the old silicone that could ooze into your body. He described the consistency of the newer silicone as safer and much more natural than any that had come before.

Wiley and I both held silicone and saline implants in our hands that day in early 2016, to feel the difference. I would later live with breast expanders for a little over three months as my breast tissue and muscle were expanded out with saline and I hated the way they felt… like water balloons. The silicone felt so much more real than the saline and my plastic surgeon told me they were just as safe as the saline, so I eventually chose those.

I also remember a quick discussion about capsular contracture, but we were told that it was also very rare and nothing to worry about. That plastic surgery consultation was extremely positive and we both left there feeling good about my decision to reconstruct with implants since there didn't seem to be any issues what so ever that would cause me to have problems.

I had done a bit of research online about breast implants, but didn't come across much. I remember looking at the FDA website, but there weren't very many implant complaints compared to the sheer number of women that had them.

At the time, I was involved with my breast cancer treatment and put far more trust in my doctors than I would have if I hadn't been in the middle of trying to survive cancer. There is such a major learning curve when you are diagnosed with cancer. So many decisions to be made and so many options to choose from. I had moved forward with reconstruction after both breasts were removed because I wanted my breasts back and implants seemed like the most reasonable and safe way to do that. The focus after I survived cancer naturally changed to getting an aesthetically pleasing substitute for what I had lost.

My friends and family were all in support and even joked that I would now have a new set of breasts back up where they used to be. They were the silver lining to a terrible experience and everywhere I went women supported that idea. Even cancer support groups were supporting and advocating for reconstruction. I was never offered flat as an option by any medical professional, because breasts were considered the best way to go after cancer and that seemed reasonable at the time, especially considering I was still in my forties.

I only knew one woman that had not done reconstruction after her double mastectomy and gone straight to flat. I wish I had spent more time talking to her about her decision, but looking back if there was a "natural" way to regain breasts without any side effects, why the heck not!

I had heard about the breast implant lawsuits in the 1990's, but I was in my early twenties at the time and had no interest in breast implants. My twenty-something breasts were in great shape and I loved them. I never imagined that I would someday need implants, so I didn't pay much attention. I do remember my grandparents talking about their neighbor's son losing his Santa Barbara based breast implant company to lawsuits, but it didn't affect me, so I ignored it decades earlier.

Nicole Daruda, the founder of *Healing Breast Implant Illness* had been through this struggle herself and had made it her mission to inform and educate women about the reality of breast implants and the damage they can do. Her social media presence and website were a wealth of information. I vacillated between panic and anger as I realized that my symptoms mirrored those on the list Nicole had created. *Did I have breast implant illness (BII)? Why had I never heard of it until now? Was it real?*

A lot of the BII symptoms could be attributed to other illnesses, diseases, or pharmaceuticals, but I found it very compelling that most of the women in the group did not have the symptoms or issues until after they received their implants. Furthermore, in the majority of cases some or all of the symptoms and issues resolved after explant (removal of the breast implants). The stories were not limited to breast implants and women also complained of the same symptoms with butt implants, chin implants, pectoral implants and other foreign objects placed inside the body.

After reading up on BII for over a week I suspected that it was the cause of all of my health issues, but I needed proof. I had kept a journal and taken lots of notes at every doctor's appointment I went to from my 2015 diagnosis to present day. I pulled out all of my handwritten notes and organized the hundreds of breast photos taken by my husband, Wiley, to guide me through this new investigation.

As I looked back at that time of treatment and healing, I realized that the symptoms came on one by one and at a pace that kept me from linking them all together. It felt plausible at the time that all of my symptoms were related to breast cancer and the treatment and surgeries I had endured. That theory was being confirmed by all of my doctors, so it seemed plausible. Armed with a lot of new information and looking back with a fresh set of eyes, my current reality began to come into focus.

Sunshine suggested that I speak to her friend, Talia Krainock Maddock, who had been the one to introduce her to BII. Talia lived in Texas and Sunshine organized for us to have a phone chat one afternoon. Talia had a terrible reaction to her implants and shared the details of her struggle with BII and explant. She really helped me wrap my head around everything I had learned. She encouraged me to start the search for an explant surgeon and get them removed as soon as possible. After speaking with Talia, it confirmed to me that BII was real and was causing the majority of my symptoms. I am continually blown away by the strength, openness, and community that evolves when women work together to educate others about their experiences. Speaking to Talia and finding my voice soon after to write this book felt like a nod from the universe that I was on the right track even though some days it felt like I had lost my way.

Chapter Four
Understanding BII

How could breast implants cause such a myriad of symptoms and what is breast implant illness? As I found out from personal experience, there is no one medical test for confirming BII. I searched out the information on the internet as no doctor I consulted seemed to know much about it, some had never even heard of it.

According to the information provided by *Healing Breast Implant Illness* and the experiences of over 100,000 women on their corresponding Facebook page, there are a myriad of reasons why the body reacts to implants.

Firstly, they are huge foreign objects and the body recognizes and attacks them as such. Secondly, they are made up of a list of shockingly toxic substances including heavy metals that are considered dangerous to the human body. Thirdly, one of the largest studies in September 2018 concluded that silicone implants are associated with rare harmful and serious diseases.[v]

Healing Breast Implant Illness states that "They can affect most body systems, symptoms are widespread and can be related to chemical and heavy metal toxicity, bio toxicity, immune dysfunction, auto-immune symptoms, neurological symptoms, endocrine symptoms and metabolic symptoms."[vi] The evidence is highlighted in multiple studies and more information is coming to light all the time. I would encourage you to educate yourself using the *Resources* page at the end of this book to seek out all of the detailed information available as there is far too much to tackle here.

The following possible symptoms were listed on the *Healing Breast Implant Illness* webpage and could be caused by a multitude of autoimmune diseases and/or reactions to all kinds of things including the aromatase inhibitors prescribed after breast cancer treatment ends.[vii] I wasn't currently taking pharmaceuticals of any kind, so I was immediately able to rule that out as a possible culprit. The 🌸 next to each one indicates a symptom that I was personally experiencing as a result of my silicone breast implants.

Breast Implant Illness Symptoms

🌸 FATIGUE
🌸 BRAIN FOG
🌸 MEMORY LOSS
🌸 MUSCLE AND JOINT PAIN
🌸 HAIR LOSS, DRY SKIN AND HAIR
🌸 PREMATURE AGING
🌸 WEIGHT PROBLEMS
🌸 INFLAMMATION
🌸 POOR SLEEP AND INSOMNIA

- DRY EYES, DECLINE IN VISION
- HYPO/HYPER THYROID SYMPTOMS
- HYPO/HYPER ADRENAL SYMPTOMS
- PARATHYROID PROBLEMS
- HORMONE IMBALANCE, DIMINISHING HORMONES
- EARLY MENOPAUSE, HYSTERECTOMY
- LOW LIBIDO
- SLOW HEALING, EASY BRUISING
- THROAT CLEARING, COUGH, DIFFICULTY SWALLOWING, CHOKING, REFLUX, METALLIC TASTES
- VERTIGO
- GASTROINTESTINAL ISSUES SUCH AS ACID REFLUX, GERD, GASTRITIS
- LEAKY GUT, IBS AND SIBO
- PANCREATITIS
- FEVERS, NIGHT SWEATS, INTOLERANT TO HEAT/COLD
- PERSISTENT BACTERIAL, VIRAL, FUNGAL INFECTIONS
- YEAST, CANDIDA, SINUS AND UTI INFECTIONS
- SKIN RASHES
- EAR RINGING
- SUDDEN FOOD INTOLERANCE AND ALLERGIES
- HEADACHES, MIGRANES AND OCULAR MIGRANES
- SLOW MUSCLE RECOVERY AFTER ACTIVITY
- HEART PALPITATIONS
- CHANGES IN NORMAL HEART RATE OR HEART PAIN
- SORE AND ACHING JOINTS OF SHOULDERS, HIPS, BACKBONE, HANDS AND FEE
- SWOLLEN AND TENDER LYMPH NODES IN BREAST AREA, UNDERARM, THROAT, NECK, GROIN
- DEHYDRATION FOR NO REASON
- FREQUENT URINATION
- NUMBNESS/TINGLING SENSATION IN UPPER AND LOWER LIMBS
- COLD AND DISCOLORED LIMBS, HANDS AND FEET
- GENERAL CHEST DISCOMFORT SHORTNESS OF BREATH

- PAIN AND OR BURNING SENSATION AROUND IMPLANT AND OR UNDERARM
- LIVER AND KIDNEY DYSFUNCTION
- GALLBLADDER PROBLEMS
- TOXIC SHOCK SYMPTOMS
- ANXIETY, DEPRESSION AND PANIC ATTACKS
- FEELING LIKE YOU ARE DYING
- SYMPTOMS OF FIBROMYALGIA
- SYMPTOMS OF LYME DISEASE
- SYMPTOMS OF EBV
- SYMPTOMS OF AUTO-IMMUNE DISEASES SUCH AS; RAYNAUD'S SYNDROME, HASHIMOTO'S THYROIDITIS, RHEUMATOID ARTHRITIS, SCLERODERMA, LUPUS, SJOGREN'S SYNDROME, NONSPECIFIC CONNECTIVE TISSUE DISEASE, MULTIPLE SCLEROSIS
- SYMPTOMS OF BIA-ALCL LYMPHOMA
- DIAGNOSIS OF CANCER

One of the ways I was able to find out if this was actually BII caused by my implants was to take all of my symptoms and the dates that I started complaining about them and lay them all into a timeline to see if anything stood out. I was shocked by what I discovered. It had NEVER dawned on me, that all of my symptoms began after my breast implants had been placed. The following timeline I created laid out the undeniable facts.

Timeline of My Symptoms and Complaints

* 5/18/16   Breast tissue expander surgery to get my chest ready for breast implants

* 5/18 to 8/17/16   Seromas developed in each armpit as a result of the expanders. The first sign that my body was reacting to having foreign objects in my body, but I was told it was normal

* 8/17/16   Surgery to remove expanders and replace with silicone implants. Seromas removed with liposuction during the surgery

* 10/4/16   Quarterly oncology appointment. Complained about new leg & foot pain

* 10/4/17   Weight 156 pounds

* 1/08/17   AWS (Axillary web syndrome) painful cording developed in my chest and abdomen that was not there after the double mastectomy

* 1/10/17   Quarterly oncology appointment, complained about worsening joint/muscle pain and stiffness

* 9/13/17   Complained to Primary Care Physician of new allergies and sinus issues

* 9/28/18   Weight 161 pounds

* 10/12/18   Diagnosed with my very first UTI (urinary tract infection) and treated with antibiotics

- 11/14/18   Quarterly appointment with oncologist, lots of new symptoms and complaints including, anxiety, exhaustion, shortness of breath, muscle aches, heart palpitations, bruising easily, food intolerances, sinus congestion, feeling bloated and gassy, and insomnia.

- 12/4 to 2/20/18   Infrared sauna (10 sessions - 45 minutes each) to relieve symptoms, but they worsened

- 11/15/18   First mammogram to check on implants and investigate new breast pain and discomfort

- 12/25/18   Christmas Day; sharp, severe left breast pain that took my breath away and I had to lay down.

- 01/09/19   Weight 167 pounds
- 01/10/19   Cardiology appointment, complaining about heart palpitations and shooting pain in my left arm and left side

- 01/18/19   Completely healed left breast incision opens up and bleeds after 2 years and 5 months for no reason, possible breast infection

As I looked at the timeline I had made for my symptoms, I discovered that only two months after the expanders were swapped out for the breast implants I began to complain about joint and muscle pain that hadn't been there before the implants. I was in my late forties, but my body felt like it was rapidly aging.

Only four months after placement, I developed very painful cording in my chest and abdomen. I was told it was AWS (Axillary web syndrome) and I my physical therapist would physically break the cords which left me bruised and sore.

After a little over two years, I began to experience panic and anxiety attacks for the first time in my life. They would come on without warning and usually accompanied by a hot flash that felt like being buried in molten lava. They were unbearable and becoming more and more frequent.

At about the same time, I began to experience insomnia that plagued me nightly. I woke up every morning feeling like I hadn't slept soundly all night. There was also a constant feeling of pressure in my chest that wouldn't allow me to take a deep breath. If I tried to exercise or do anything strenuous, I would feel short of breath and would need to sit or lay down to recover.

I was starting to notice physical changes to my body after the two-year mark including an eleven-pound weight gain. I hadn't changed my eating habits and was exercising, but the weight just kept coming. Unexplained pain and soreness developed around both implants and in the tissue between them and around my sternum. The pain on my left side began to affect my left arm and it was hard to raise it above my head.

All of these symptoms and dozens more from the list got worse over time and culminated in an overall feeling that I was dying. It was similar to what I experienced during chemotherapy, but had gone away after it was completed. This feeling wouldn't leave. Some days I thought it would have been better if cancer had taken my life as I felt overwhelmed and sick. I thought about taking my own life to end the pain and anguish, but I wanted to live and I could not fathom the pain and devastation that act would bring to everyone that knew me. I had to figure out what was wrong with me, but none of my doctors were providing any clues.

My sisters questioned whether I was depressed, but I knew in my heart that I wasn't, because I loved my life and wanted nothing more than to get back to it. Before breast cancer and breast implants I woke up every morning feeling refreshed and glad to be alive. I looked forward to every new day and most days I woke up and would sing while I got ready. Something was wrong, because I was silenced and I didn't know why.

I hurt all over and I just wanted some sort of relief. I had already tried acupuncture, detoxing in an infrared sauna, adding and deleting foods from my diet, removing caffeine, adding in CBD and cannabis products for insomnia, taking various minerals and supplements in the hopes my body would start to heal itself. I continued to press all of my doctors for answers, but nobody had any. I think they probably though I was a little crazy. I presented with a whole lot of unexplained symptoms that didn't seem to be backed up by any blood tests. On paper, I was healthy, but I was suffering and deep down I knew that there was something really wrong with me. *If it wasn't a cancer reoccurrence, what was it?*

I had also started to notice that my reconstructed breasts were physically changing shape. They had been so perfectly symmetrical for the first couple of years and looked damn good, but they didn't look like the perfect photos anymore. They were also beginning to feel tighter in my chest, almost like having hard oranges placed under my skin.

By Christmas of 2018, there was no ignoring the extremely tight implants in my chest and the pain and discomfort in the tissue surrounding both breasts. All of the tissue around the implants themselves was sore to the touch. The discomfort radiated out from both breasts to include my sternum, my abdomen, under both armpits, and into both arms. Some days it hurt to even lightly touch my skin and my clothing brushing my chest made me wince.

My left breast scar near my armpit was visibly starting to pucker and draw inward. The right breast looked flat on the side nearest my armpit. They didn't used to look like that. Something had changed for the worse. If I leaned over, my breasts didn't look right. I had sharp breast pains on and off since they were implanted, but the pains were so fleeting, I figured my breast implants must be settling in like an old house with creaky floor boards.

February 13, 2019 - Photo shows my left breast, near my arm, pulling in slightly toward my body and my right breast was swollen larger than the left, a known symptom of ALCL

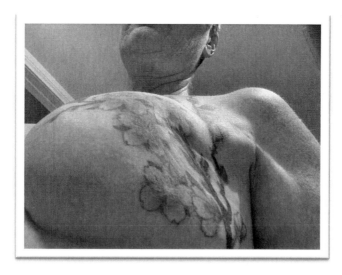

March 28th, 2019 (6 weeks later) - You can see the breast tissue has pulled in even further leaving a dent and flat area on my left breast with a small bulge into the armpit

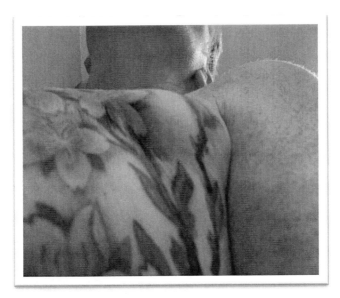

May 3rd, 2019 (5 weeks later) - The dent had pulled in so
much that the bulge in my left breast was much bigger

When I leaned forward, both breasts became very flat on the sides
and were misshapen. The diagnosis was capsular contracture.

After spending an entire week in February 2019 investigating all of this new information, I felt overwhelmed and couldn't get all of the questions and new-found facts to stop swirling around in my head. Wiley was gone on his business trip, so I found myself in our teenager's room needing someone to talk to and process the chaos I was feeling. Vance patiently listened to everything I had to say about my breast implants, the symptoms I was experiencing, and the timeline of their appearance. After I had shared all of my new discoveries, Vance looked at me and then said in a very matter of fact way, "You've got to get them out." *Holy crap, he was right!*

If you have implants and are concerned about them, create a timeline of your personal symptoms and complaints. On the following pages, you can get a clearer picture of the possibility that you may be suffering from breast implant illness by logging any related events like surgery, pain, weight gain or any unexplained symptoms or issues that could be related to your implants. The log can also help you to communicate your concerns to medical professionals.

Log of Personal Symptoms & Complaints

Date	Symptom or Event	Notes

Chapter Five
Planning to Explant

Thankfully, Sunshine had joined me to the *Breast Implant Illness and Healing by Nicole* Facebook group and my mystery symptoms all started to make sense. I knew after only 24 hours that I wanted to deconstruct my breasts and get the implants out as soon as possible. I already had breast cancer and the idea that I had put implants into my chest cavity that were not only causing me over forty awful symptoms but could also cause a cancer of my immune system was truly terrifying. While researching BII, I came across a lot of information about ALCL too.

The ALCL cancer is not breast cancer, it is a cancer of the immune system directly caused by the implants themselves and the bodies response to them. I didn't really think I had to worry about the possibility of contracting ALCL, because it was caused by textured implants. I had the smooth implants as promised by my plastic surgeon, but then I saw a post that talked about textured expanders causing ALCL too. I had textured expanders for almost four months when I first started my reconstruction, so I was at risk because the scar capsule that had surrounded the expanders was still in my body and now covered the smooth implants. I had seen estimates ranging from 1 in 30,000 to Facebook groups saying the chances of contracting ALCL was closer to 1 in 2,000.

When swapping out expanders for implants I found out that it was fairly common practice among plastic surgeons to open up a patient that had expanders and pull them out of the scar capsule that the body created around them. The scar capsule was already formed, so surgeons put the new implant right into that scar capsule and would close you back up. The problem with this practice is that the scar capsule is the cause of the ALCL cancer, so leaving it inside the body continues the risk indefinitely. Finding a qualified plastic surgeon to remove the implants and scar capsules is a priority when explanting or replacing your implants.

I was also concerned that I might have ALCL due to the textured expanders that I had in my chest for four months. I asked for a copy of my surgeon's report from my original plastic surgeon to find out what had occurred during the swap of my expanders for implants. I realized that the scar capsules that formed around the Allergan textured expanders were still in my chest. My implants had been put right into the already formed capsules. I had swelling and pain off and on in both breasts which are possible symptoms of the lymphoma.

The only way to find out if you have ALCL is to have either the scar capsules tested, enlarged lymph nodes, or any fluid that surrounds the capsules. There are specific requirements about how much fluid is needed, so if there isn't any fluid you have to test the capsules. A lot of plastic surgeons leave the capsules inside the patient when they remove the implants, so those patients could contract ALCL even after the implants are removed. Patients are told the capsules will naturally break down in the body, but they don't.

The only test available for ALCL is called CD30 immune staining testing which is looking for a specific tumor marker associated with that lymphoma. There are no blood tests or any other type of testing to confirm ALCL. If you have had implants or expanders of any kind you should ask your doctor if you should have this testing done. Most plastic surgeons that know about and understand ALCL will offer the testing without argument.

That wasn't my only worry about the implants in my chest. The website that corresponded with the *Healing Breast Implant Illness* Facebook page had a current list of approved plastic surgeons that would safely explant the toxic offenders and believe you weren't crazy. I looked the list over only to find there wasn't an approved surgeon in the California desert. I phoned around and spoke to numerous plastic surgeon's offices in my area, but was unable to find one with enough explant experience to remove my implants according to the guidelines recommended.

It was late February 2019 and the number of members on the breast implant illness Facebook page was growing daily. I wasn't the only woman to decide to explant. Qualified plastic surgeons all over the United States were booking up fast for explant consultations and surgeries. Just like me, Sunshine had been introduced to BII by a friend and the information was being shared via social media at the speed of light.

Since there wasn't anyone nearby I knew I would have to travel to explant. I phoned several plastic surgeons on the list and found that some were booked out over a year and I knew I couldn't wait that long. I continued my search and found a surgeon, four hours away and considered one of the top explant surgeons in California, Dr. Roee Rubinstein. He was located in Thousand Oaks, not far from Ojai and our old stomping grounds and he was highly regarded by previous patients. I booked Dr. Rubinstein's next available consultation appointment in late March, 6 weeks out, and crossed my fingers that they would have a cancellation and I would be able to get in sooner.

While I waited for my consultation, the pain in my left breast and arm became excruciating. It was the high season in the desert and almost impossible to get a doctor's appointment, but I managed to get myself in with the physician's assistant (PA) at my primary care physician's office that same day. I explained what was going on with my breasts and that I intended to remove the breast implants as soon as possible. The PA seemed baffled and had never heard of BII, but confirmed I had a lot of swelling and inflammation and prescribed me Naproxen© to help relieve it. He was also concerned that I could possibly have an internal breast infection since the incision had opened up and bled a little several months earlier. He gave me an antibiotic to take as a precaution. He also gave me a prescription for nerve pain. Basically, he had no idea what was going on and threw three prescriptions at me hoping something might help. He also thought it would be a good idea to see my oncologist just in case something more serious was going on.

My oncologist was booked up for weeks and my next scheduled quarterly appointment was a month away. I felt very strongly at this point that I needed to be seen and heard by my doctors as soon as possible. I managed to get in to see the nurse at her office the next day. I reiterated everything I had learned about BII and all of the pain and discomfort I had been experiencing. Like the PA, she was concerned that my incision had popped open and the pain and discomfort I was having might be from an infection or an adverse reaction to the implants. She referred me to a general surgeon the next week to get a second opinion about what was going on.

I spent the next week trying not to panic and go to the worst-case scenario. It isn't uncommon for breast cancer survivors to worry that any new issues are in fact a reoccurrence of their breast cancer and I was feeling the stress. Best to get it ruled out.

The general surgeon said I was definitely having an "adverse reaction" to the implants and that I most likely had capsular contracture as well. He agreed that removing the implants would be the best option and warned me about replacing them. He was sure that my body would have the same autoimmune reaction, so he was glad to hear I was determined to go flat. *Wow, so medical professionals do know about this!*

Implants are foreign objects and the body treats them as such. As soon as a breast implant is put inside the chest your body starts to build a capsule of scar tissue around the implant to protect you from it. It is the natural way your body deals with all foreign objects. It doesn't matter if you have saline or silicone. All women have scar capsules develop around their implants and the thickness of the capsules depends on the person and the length of time they are inside you.

In my case, the capsules were thickening and tightening around the shell of the implants causing capsular contracture. Capsular contracture can tighten around the implants so much that they can cause the implant to become deformed, change shape, and even rupture. According to the Association of Plastic Surgeons, capsular contracture is a normal part of healing and 75% of cases will develop in the first two years of the implants being placed.[viii] I was just passed two years when I really started to realize something was wrong and yet, I had originally been told that it wasn't very common.

Luckily, Dr. Rubinstein's office phoned and bumped up my consultation a whole month early to February 25th. Things were moving quicker than I thought they would and I was so relieved. Waking up every morning and looking down at the silicone bags sitting over my vital organs and heart was a tough pill to swallow. I was experiencing feelings of fear and shame, because I had chosen to put the implants in my body that were now making me sick.

My original decision was based on my own vanity and ego, but it was also based on the lack of information given to me at the time. I wished I had known all of this information before I chose implants, because I would have been more informed and I would have most likely not chosen them to begin with. I could have had one surgery and been done with all of it! I went from totally in love with my implants and tattoos to wanting a divorce almost overnight!

Wiley was unable to join me for my consultation with Dr. Rubinstein, but once again, thanks to Nicole Daruda, I arrived at my appointment armed with a list of questions downloaded from her website. It wasn't the first time a woman had shown up to his office with all of the information and I was so relieved to find that he knew all about BII and believed in it. He examined me and agreed that I was suffering from a combination of capsular contracture and BII and the way to fix it was to explant.

If I chose to explant I still had the original reconstruction options to choose from. Just like my first plastic surgeon, Dr. Rubinstein offered the DIEP procedure as an option to create new breasts. It was still a long surgery and had a lengthy recovery along with the documented high rate of possible complications. I couldn't stomach the idea of more cutting and pasting to fulfill the need for breasts, so just like I had done in 2015, I declined it as a possibility.

I had an epiphany that my breasts had already been removed in 2015 and the breasts I had now felt like imposters. I wanted to get back to my true self with the least amount of complications and downtime. I desperately wanted my life back.

Dr. Rubinstein also offered fat transfer as an option to build a very small breast using my own fatty tissue that would be removed with liposuction and then placed in my chest cavity. Once again, there was the possibility of complications and tissue necrosis (tissue death), plus most of the tissue would not stay in place and additional fat transfer surgeries would most likely be needed. here was also no research studies about fat transfer, so that did not fit in with my plan either. I had undergone liposuction in my armpit area during my original implant placement surgery, because I had developed seromas, pockets of fluid, that were bulging and unsightly. The liposuction recovery was horrendously painful and I swore I would never elect to do that again unless it was absolutely necessary.

As Dr. Rubinstein and I talked, my vision for my chest became clearer. Well, actually flatter. As tempted as I was to try and recreate some form of breasts on the front of me, I knew in my gut that I needed to let them go once and for all.

My real breasts had tried to kill me and my fake ones made me sick! It was time to go flat and put the need for boobs to rest for good. He agreed that he could reconstruct me to flat, but that my cherry blossom tattoos would not make it through intact. He was concerned about how they would look and took a lot of time explaining how he would work around them as much as possible.

We also discussed my desire for lab testing on my scar capsules and my chest cavity. I had read horror stories online about molds, fungus, and bacteria growing inside the chest pockets of women that had implants. Dr. Rubinstein agreed to test my scar capsules once they were removed and swab my chest cavity. He said he would send everything off to the lab just to put my mind at ease. I knew having ALCL was a long shot, but I didn't want to look back and wish I had done the testing, but didn't. The lab testing would not be covered by my insurance, but Wiley and I agreed we were willing to pay the extra couple hundred dollars to the lab for peace of mind. My lab testing was fairly reasonable compared to the thousands of dollars that some labs charge for the exact same testing. Be sure to speak to the lab in advance of your explant surgery for a quote.

I had set up consultation appointments with three other plastic surgeons, but after spending almost an hour with Dr. Rubinstein, I knew that he was the one to safely remove my implants and reconstruct me to flat. He was not only a Harvard graduate, but a board certified plastic surgeon, a microsurgeon, and he specialized in the very complicated and detailed surgery of the hands. I could tell that with his level of experience and caring, I would get the results I wanted. I told him to move forward with my insurance company and I cancelled the other consultations on the drive back home to the desert.

Since I was a breast cancer survivor and the explant surgery was considered medically necessary, it would be covered by my insurance. If I was considering removing breast implants that had been put in for cosmetic reasons only, insurance would not pay and I would have had to pay the entire explant cost, which can go upwards of $20,000 depending on where you live.

I hadn't taken any photos of my breasts before I became aware of breast implant illness in February 2019, because we had documented everything for *Bittersweet* and I had no intention of writing a second book about my breasts. I assumed they would stay perfect and allow me to move on with my life and in 8-10 years, I would have these taken out and a new set put in. That seems so unrealistic knowing what I know now.

Dr. Rubinstein was very clear at my appointment that he could not guarantee that all of my BII symptoms would go away after my implants were removed because there was a possibility that some of them were being caused by something else. He was also clear about the fact that even though I wanted this to be my very last breast surgery there was always the possibility that I might need a revision for one reason or another. I appreciated how truthful he was about the whole process and he didn't downplay any of it.

Two days after seeing Dr. Rubinstein for my explant and reconstruction consultation I took an ANA blood test for my Primary Care Physician. She wanted to rule out the possibility that I had an autoimmune disease that could be the culprit of some of my symptoms. An ANA blood test looks for antinuclear antibodies in the blood. The immune system normally makes antibodies to fight infection, but if you test positive for antinuclear antibodies it means your body could be attacking its own tissues. If you have a positive ANA test it indicates that your body has launched a misdirected attack on your own tissue and you are having an autoimmune response. Further testing will be needed to pinpoint exactly what autoimmune disease you are suffering from, an ANA is just the beginning. [ix]

I was surprised to receive a negative ANA blood test result. I had no inflammatory markers even though I was suffering from a lot of the symptoms. This was great news because it meant that I had not developed an autoimmune disease while I had the breast implants but something was still very wrong with me and the implants had to be the cause.

Chapter Six
Four Weeks Out from Explant

The need to escape my current reality was palpable. Every few hours a wave of fight-or-flight accompanied a hot flash that burned from the inside out. It would slowly rise and strengthen to the point that I could not hold back the tears or the sense of overwhelming panic that was inside me. I could not catch my breath or think straight as my heartbeat would race and all hope escaped me. I had never experienced anxiety like this and wondered if I might be losing my mind. Post after post on Nicole's Facebook page confirmed that I was not alone in this. There were now over 70,000 women members in the group feeling and sharing exactly what I was going through. This was not all in my mind, it was a result of my body reacting to foreign objects and the chemicals in them.

When another wave of anxiety started to rise, I learned to invite it in, take a deep breath and allow the panic to penetrate every cell in my body. I knew that if I didn't resist, it would not persist. Like the tides, it washed in and slowly out, leaving me feeling tired, beaten, and lifeless. I would recover by either having to sit or lay down only to experience it a short time later. Again, and again, all day, every day. It was relentless.

I knew that I needed to explant the toxic source of my anxiety, but was fearful that going through another major surgery would not solve all of my symptoms. Not only that, but it was very likely that my cherry blossom tattoos that I absolutely loved would be completely ruined leaving a mess of bright colored ink on my chest. *What if I deconstructed my beautiful reconstructed breasts and nothing changed?* It was my biggest fear, but I had no choice. I couldn't live like that.

We waited two weeks to get approval from my insurance before being given a surgery date. Dr. Rubinstein was booking out a couple months, so we took the next available surgery date, Friday, May 17th, 2019. I would be the first patient of the day, checking in at 5:45 am and surgery scheduled for 7:00 am. The need to get my health and life back grew daily and May 17th could not come soon enough. Wiley rearranged his work schedule to take time off to care for me… again.

As I waited for my surgery date, I began to write this book. It was clear that the way *Bittersweet* ended, with my beautiful tattooed chest and renewed zest for life was clearly not the end of the story. I also had feelings of guilt for promoting breast implants and reconstruction when in reality, it had all gone wrong for me after the book was published. I knew that some women would still choose implants and reconstruction, but I felt that they should be armed with all of the information when making that choice.

I dove head first into the open waters of the internet, swimming from site to site, swallowing more pool water than was good for me. I was obsessed. It was a healthy obsession brought on by the need to make sure that this time around, I knew everything about breast implant illness and that I was properly explanting to rid myself of the symptoms.

A list of toxic ingredients made its way up and down my Facebook feed. I had never been told what chemicals made up the shell or inside of the silicone implants I lived with every day. Implants were presented to me as the best option after a double mastectomy because they were only made of silicone. The Allergan breast implant brochure given to me after they were put in said, "We use silicone every day. Silicones are made from silicon, a naturally occurring element found in sand, quartz and rock. Next to oxygen, silicon is the most common element in the earth's crust, and becomes silicone when it is combined with oxygen, carbon and hydrogen."[x]

Sounds harmless enough. *What could be so toxic about that?* The list of ingredients below will answer that for you. This is only a list of known ingredients that make up the shell and inner core of a breast implant that was revealed during the Dow Chemical Breast Implant Trial.[xi] Each make and model of implant varies, but the reaction your body can have to the chemically laden toxic implants isn't surprising if you spend a little time googling the effect of each chemical on the human body. To my knowledge there are no long-term studies focusing on breast implants and the effect of a 98.6-degree body on them. The FDA has admitted that implants "bleed" small amounts of silicone and heavy metals through the intact shell of the implant into the body.[xii] The implants do not have to be ruptured for this to happen. At the time that I was choosing implants, there was no requirement by the FDA to disclose harmful ingredients in breast implants even though there was evidence they can cause illness. CRAZY!

Known Ingredients of Breast Implants[xiii]

- Methyl ethyl ketone (neurotoxin)
- Cyclohexanone (neurotoxin)
- Isopropyl Alcohol
- Denatured Alcohol
- Acetone (used in nail polish remover and is a neurotoxin)
- Urethane
- Polyvinyl chloride (neurotoxin)
- Amine
- Toluene
- Dichloromethane (carcinogen)
- Chloromethane
- Ethyl acetate (neurotoxin)
- Silicone
- Sodium fluoride
- Lead Based Solder
- Formaldehyde
- Talcum powder
- Oakite (cleaning solvent)
- Methyl 2- Cyanoacrylates
- Ethylene Oxide (Carcinogen)
- Xylene (neurotoxin)
- Hexon

- 2-Hedanone
- Thixon-OSN-2
- Stearic Acid
- Zinc Oxide
- Naphtha (rubber solvent)
- Phenol (neurotoxin)
- Benzene (carcinogen/neurotoxin)
- Lacquer thinner
- Epoxy resin
- Epoxy hardener
- Printing Ink
- Metal cleaning acid
- Color pigments as release agents
- Heavy metals such as aluminum (neurotoxin linked to Alzheimer's and auto immune disorders)
- Platinum
- Silica

The list of ingredients was shocking, but it really wasn't that shocking that my plastic surgeon never disclosed them to me. *Can you imagine that conversation?* I am 100% sure that I would have left that consultation with a hell-no attitude toward breast implants. I also wonder if my plastic surgeon was ever provided a list of what was in the implants. It seems like the manufacturers would want to keep their toxic secret, because it could damage their very profitable industry.

What medical device sales person would want to divulge that? None! So, I am left to believe that the lack of transparency and lack of truthful information begins with the manufacturer, it spreads down through their organization to their sales people, then it is spread out to the plastic surgeons that purchase their products, and finally the lack of any kind of truthful warning is not passed onto the patient or their insurance company (deep pockets), because let's face it... this is a billion-dollar industry and money matters more than our lives. *Shocking?* Not so much. The manufacturers had help. They didn't perpetrate this deception on women worldwide alone.

As I kept reading the posts on Facebook about breast implant illness, I started to learn that these problems have been around for decades. The Dow Corning lawsuits in the 1990's was about these very same issues and resulted in breast implants being removed from the market by the FDA in 1992, only to be allowed back on that same year for breast reconstruction in clinical studies.[xiv] They were allowed back on the market in the early 2000's for everyone with the promise of long term clinical studies by the manufacturers.

Silicone implants had damaged thousands of women, but they were somehow safe to continue to put into women that had just gone through cancer? Really? I believe the FDA failed to protect American women from the harm of breast implants when they allowed breast implants back on the market without sufficient safety studies and without knowing their long-term effects.

After my implants were placed in my body, I was given a slick brochure with pictures of young, beautiful women that had perfect breasts. I now know that the brochure was probably part of the box that held my implants and other device information that was to be given to me the patient. It seems this information would be pertinent before implantation, but I am not the only patient to receive the information in a brochure form after it is a moot point, because they are already inside of me!

The brochure I was given talks about the history of breast implants along with other important possible symptom information that would have been useful in making the decision in the first place. They use facts to their advantage, "Silicone gel-filled implants are among the most studied medical devices. They are the subject of literally thousands of studies and published reports."[xv] Just because there are thousands of studies does not make something safe.

Hindsight is 20/20, but what if I had been given all of the information before I chose to reconstruct with implants? Well, I am pretty certain that I would have felt differently than I do now. I would not feel deceived, angry, and lied to about the safety and hazards of the implants that I have to worry about every day. Withholding information about a medical device prevents the patient from making informed consent. My plastic surgeon at the time of implant was realistic and honest about the possible complications and hazards of the actual surgery, but not about the possible side effects of the devices about to be implanted inside my chest.

After googling to exhaustion and spending months on the internet reading devastating story after devastating story, I needed a break. Wiley and I packed up our car for a brief vacation in the Joshua Tree National Park to get away from our current reality. After arriving at the campground, Wiley set up the shade tent with lounge chairs and went to work building what would be our home base for the next 24 hours. It was so quiet and the desert wind clean and cool. It was only a little over an hour from our home, but felt a million miles away. Vance stayed behind to play video games and take care of our cat, Tiger. Wiley and I spent the afternoon climbing giant boulders and lounging on the flat rocks in the sun. The warmth of the sun on my back and the natural beauty of everything that surrounded us filled me once again with hope. The dread of a fifth, and hopefully, final surgery melted away as the desert sand blew through my hair.

A tiny, grey squirrel sat very still on a rock shaped like a heart. Everywhere I looked the rocks took on organic shapes. There were hearts and breasts everywhere. A voice inside me reassured me that it was all going to be alright. My life with Wiley and Vance was not one that I wanted to let go of without a fight. I had held on for dear life during all of the trials and tribulations of the last three years of my cancer drama. I wasn't ready to leave and yet I knew that it was completely out of my hands. I would go if I was meant to and in reality, I didn't want to go kicking and screaming out of this life and into the next realm. So, I tried to prepare myself for every eventuality.

I'm not crazy, they look like boobs, right?

The eventuality that no one ever wants to prepare for is death. I tried to allow the peace that I know death would bring be a possibility. I didn't want to go, but I felt that both my parents, John and Carol, would be waiting for me on the other side, so if it was meant to be, I would be so happy to see them. It had been almost 20 years since my dad's sudden death to a heart attack and almost 17 since my mother died of cancer. Neither parent did any medical as they were devout Christian Scientists and prayer was all they thought they needed. I missed them terribly. Fifty years of this current life seemed like an eternity and simultaneously just a moment in time.

Always the optimist, thank you Christian Science (I am being sarcastic) I had to wonder, what if I could live into my eighties or nineties. Would that even be possible considering my genetic mutations and past battle with cancer? I guess I would just have to choose to live fully and in every moment and hope for the best.

The sun started to set over the enormous boulders that were the backdrop of our campsite. Wiley lit the campfire and the heat rose upward and out from the fire pit. The English Beat played quietly in the background as the wind whipped the shade tent, "Mirror in the bathroom please don't break…" Wiley poured me a glass of French rosé from Provence as we waited for our friends to arrive with their kids and fill the campsite with life. I needed to let go and stop myself from overthinking. This was the perfect place to do it. It's let go time… explant surgery here I come.

Joshua Tree National Park was filled with rocks
shaped like hearts and I was feeling the love!

Chapter Seven
BII Hits the Mainstream

Thankfully, social media had jolted me into reality and I knew exactly what was wrong with me and what I needed to do to fix it. I had come to believe that my breast implants, were literally poisoning my body and creating an autoimmune response like no other I had experienced. From morning to night, my body fought the two foreign objects that were in my chest leaving me with hardly any energy left to live my life. The only way to stop the poisoning was to remove the toxic silicone implants.

I had learned so much about BII and had a hard time shaking the anger and resentment I felt toward an entire industry that had not only supported me getting them, but hid the truth about their side effects. I had chosen breast implants after breast cancer and I felt used, victimized, and betrayed, but I wasn't the only one. The BII Facebook group continued to grow to over 80,000 members all trying to make sense of the information that was starting to gain traction in the media.

Due to the pressure being brought by women around the country, the FDA announced that they would be holding a two-day hearing on March 25-26, 2019 about breast implant safety and risk at their headquarters in Silver Spring, Maryland. They wanted to hear from professionals and consumers about their experiences with the devices. I logged onto the FDA Med Watch Adverse Event Reporting Program and filed an adverse reaction report pertaining to my Allergan implants. I was also encouraged by the admins on the FB group to send an email to the FDA telling my story which I did. Nothing like a little grassroots action to make you feel empowered.

It was pretty amazing how fast word started to spread and the amount of social media posts that were dedicated to the topic of BII. It was on the local news across the country and women were coming out by the thousands to talk and share their stories. It was a tremendous relief to know that the information was finally starting to be shared but at the same time it was discouraging that there were so many women blindsided by all of this information.

I started sharing information and experiences on my social media pages to help raise awareness. I knew quite a few women with breast implants, some had chosen them for cosmetic reasons and others as a result of breast cancer just like me. I felt responsible for sharing my breast implant journey as a positive one now that I had discovered it wasn't all roses. I needed to make amends and to end the cover-up.

The week of my 50th birthday, I posted a photo of my bare reconstructed and tattooed breasts to get the word out, nothing like a nipple-less photo to grab your attention and get you to read my post.

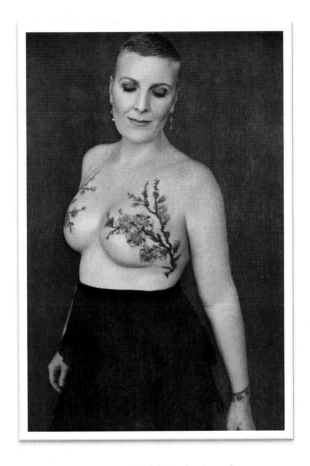

Photo by Ashleigh Taylor Portrait

After posting the photo above on social media, I was amazed at how many of my personal friends reached out to me with similar stories about mysterious symptoms and illnesses and dozens of other women I didn't even know. We felt a collective shame for allowing plastic surgeons to cut us open and implant our chests with toxic silicone shells, but the shame was short lived when we realized that we were not properly informed.

Our consent was steam rolled by an industry hell-bent on making money over women's health. As I continued my search for answers I came across study after study that revealed possible links between breast implants and autoimmune symptoms and diseases.

One of the most recent large-scale studies in 2018 was a collaboration between Israel and the University of Alberta and compared 25,000 women with breast implants to 100,000 women without breast implants. They found a 45% increase in autoimmune diseases with women that had implants over those that didn't. Sjögren's syndrome (autoimmune disorder of the salivary and tear glands), systemic sclerosis (autoimmune disorder of the connective tissue affecting the skin, arteries, and visceral organs such as lungs and kidneys) and sarcoidosis (autoimmune disorder of the lung, skin, and lymph nodes) all showed a strong association with breast implants.[xvi]

"Bottom line, there is clear evidence that implantation of foreign bodies in humans is not without risks in patients who are genetically predisposed to an autoimmune disorder. This is why screening measures, such as warning women who already have pre-existing autoimmune diseases or allergies of the increased risk, need to be put in place before surgery," says Jan Willem Cohen Tervaert, the director of the Division of Rheumatology at the University of Alberta. [xvii]

What this really means is that anyone with a family history of autoimmune disease should avoid breast implants like the plague.

That includes me. This was inevitable with my family history and yet it never came up in any conversation with any of my doctors. That wasn't the only secret being kept quiet.

On May 5, 2019, the FDA announced that they were shutting down a program that allowed medical device manufacturers to hide adverse reaction reports of malfunctions and patient harm from the general public. The "alternative summary reporting" had hidden millions, yes, millions, of adverse reaction reports for class III medical devices from the 1990's to the present day. That included all kinds of medical devices and breast implants from every manufacturer. Hundreds of thousands of women and their doctors had filed reports with the FDA about issues caused by their breast implants and the FDA had buried the information. Some of the reports documented serious injury and even death due to implants and it all remained hidden.[xviii]

If you went to the FDA website looking for adverse reports about implants prior to 2019 you would have found a couple hundred reports a year for the last couple decades. No wonder I didn't see anything alarming when I researched breast implants back in 2015, the truth was being hidden from me.

After the FDA decided to become transparent on this issue, the numbers spiked in the early months of 2019 into the thousands and continued to increase as women found out about breast implant problems and began to report their issues and bad experiences. *I was left wondering who was protecting us from unscrupulous device manufacturers if the FDA was not? Isn't that their job?*

Chapter Eight
Bye-Bye Boobs

It's funny how an experience in your childhood that you haven't thought of for ages can come flooding back like it was just yesterday. I was about thirteen years old and I had been home sick from school for more than a week covered in red, itchy bumps. I don't recall what was wrong with me and it isn't surprising because in our Christian Scientist household there was no sickness or disease, that was considered error and did not exist. Any ailments or illness would be prayed away instead of a visit to the doctor. On occasion, a childhood illness would keep us home for weeks when other kids bounced back with the aid of antibiotics or other remedies. We suffered for weeks, like it did this time.

Once I returned to school I have a very vivid memory of sitting on the school stage in the auditorium waiting to rehearse one of our Broadway style shows led by our favorite music teacher, Miss Ridilla. My close girlfriends were huddled around me in their black and white hounds-tooth school uniforms catching up on all the latest gossip. I explained to them the reason for my long absence from school. I told them about the red, itchy bumps that were all over my arms, legs, and chest and kept me in bed for far too long.

The girls were very sympathetic and expressed how glad they were that the bumps were gone and I was back in their orbit.

It was then that I realized the adolescent boys in my class had overheard and honed-in on one particular detail of my recollection. I had described small, round, bumps on my chest. They teased me relentlessly and I knew they were really talking about my very flat, undeveloped chest. They pointed at my nonexistent breasts and their laughing echoed through the theater. I was horrified! Miss Ridilla had no idea why the boys were causing such a raucous and got us all focused back on our singing and choreography. I felt embarrassed and gutted the rest of the day.

I was a late bloomer and knew this to be a fact. All I had to do was look at my younger sister, Sarah, who already at the age of eleven had a drawer full of pretty bras. My older sister, June, was fifteen and could easily fill out her shirts and dresses and had been shopping for bras for years. I was the middle child, the peacemaker and the last of the Bishop girls to develop. I wanted so badly to have the pretty bras and breasts to fill them like my sisters. I never said anything to them as I didn't want to bring more attention to my current underdevelopment.

The boy's teasing and echoing laughter pierced my young and fragile sense of self-esteem in the theater that day and dampened my usual upbeat personality. That evening at the dinner table, my mother noticed I was visibly upset, and asked me what the problem was. It was embarrassing and I didn't want to talk about it in front of my dad and two sisters, but she pushed me to share the details. My parents were our biggest cheerleaders and always supported our dreams and felt our disappointments. I knew it was a safe space to speak up, so I explained what had happened that day with the boys teasing me. I don't remember my sister's reactions, but my dad not understanding how gutted I was by the boys teasing burst out laughing and made a joke about me being flat as a board.

My incredibly supportive and loving dad had joined the boys in the ridicule of a part of my body that I had absolutely no control over. My young heart tore open and the tears began to fall uncontrollably. No young girl wants her insecurities to be confirmed by her dad, the most important man in her life. I thought that if my dad thought me being flat was funny, the boys must be right and my feelings didn't matter.

My sensitive and loving mother's voice raised louder than usual and all I remember her saying as I ran from the table was my dad's name in a very scolding tone, "John Bishop!" Tears flooded down my face as I threw my flat chest onto my bed and buried my head in my down pillows. Shortly after, my mom and dad came into my room and sat on the edge of my bed. I had soaked a portion of my pink and white floral Laura Ashley comforter with my tears and my eyes were red and swollen.

My dad apologized for his lack of sensitivity. He encouraged me not to listen to the boys and that I was perfect just the way I was. My mom gently rubbed my back and soothed my crushed ego. They both confirmed that I would grow into a beautiful woman someday and that I just needed to be patient. I wasn't sure I believed them. All I knew was that I didn't want to be flat chested. I wanted breasts. I wanted to be grown up and a woman.

I didn't even know that I was carrying around insecurities about my breast size from almost four decades earlier. This revelation brought all of the raw feelings to the surface and I was finally able to deal with them. I felt more confident than ever that I could heal those feelings of early body insecurity and embrace my flat chest again. I can tell that little girl now that her flat chest was beautiful and that in the grand scheme of things, boobs are so unimportant compared to being alive and healthy. I vowed to continue to love myself without breasts and to be proud and to feel beautiful no matter what they ended up looking like after they were reconstructed.

As my explant date neared, I was able to better handle the symptoms I was experiencing knowing that I was not alone. I could log onto Facebook and literally find tens of thousands of women to listen and support how I was feeling. Nicole's Breast Implant Illness page was gaining more members every day and by the publishing of this book had surpassed 100,000 members.

My sense of desperation eased and I began to plan and prepare for another round of cutting, swelling, discomfort, and healing. I felt confident that this would be the last surgery as a result of my breast cancer diagnosis in 2015. I was actually starting to feel giddy and excited about my implants being removed. I felt more and more confident in my decision to go flat and I just wanted to feel like myself again.

The confidence was totally opposite to how I felt when I went flat after my original double mastectomy. I was terrified then to lose my life and breasts to cancer and felt that I had no choice, but to remove them. I didn't want to die in my forties. My real breasts had tried to kill me, so I removed them. Now my fake breasts were attacking me and I was over it. I was no longer going to be a victim to cancer and fearful of being flat chested. I was going to eliminate the silicone and live my life flat, fierce, and fabulous.

The day before explant, Wiley and I checked into our hotel in Thousand Oaks. We would be staying there two nights until I was cleared for the drive home after surgery. It wasn't an ideal scenario staying in a hotel after surgery, but Dr. Rubinstein had many patients that had done it and it had worked out fine.

Since I wouldn't be home in my own bed with all of the creature comforts at hand, I brought everything I would need and then some. My biggest item was a U-shaped body pillow that was recommended by dozens of women that had explanted before me. For a few weeks after surgery it is nearly impossible to lay flat and then be able to sit up on your own, so a body pillow would support me while I slept sitting up. I wished I had known about this when I had my original double mastectomy, it would have been a life saver.

I brought extra pillows, a handmade quilt made by my friend, Teresa Perry, a cooler filled with fruit and snacks, bottled water, frozen ice packs, button front comfortable clothing, seat belt pillows for the ride home, and more. You name it, I brought it. This was the fifth surgery in three years, so I knew what I needed and Wiley was well-versed in caring for me after we left the surgery center.

This was my lounging and sleeping set up for the weeks following
explant and a second breast reconstruction surgery to make me flat.
My arms were comfortably at my sides resting on the body pillow
and I tucked the cat body pillow under my legs to support my back.
I used a memory gel neck pillow to keep my neck straight up and
down while I slept. Wiley rolled his laptop table next to my bed
at the perfect height for me to reach. I slept a lot the first couple
of weeks which definitely helped my healing

After we checked into the hotel and lugged everything to our room we met Dr. Rubinstein for my pre-op appointment. I hadn't seen him since my consultation, so it was good for Wiley to meet him and for all of us to make sure we were on the same page about what "flat" meant to me.

Requesting to be flat seems pretty obvious, but it isn't. I had read so many horror stories of women being promised by their surgeons that they would be flat with no extra skin or tissue after surgery only to wake up and find a complete mess on the front of their chests. At my breast cancer support group, several women had shown me their unacceptable flat results while we were in the women's bathrooms and others shared their photos through social media.

Some of the botched explants were downright disturbing. How a surgeon could possibly think leaving big empty pockets of skin that were sewn together and sagging on a woman's chest was mind-boggling. At my original consultation, I was very specific and explained what I expected after my explant and how I wanted to look. Dr. Rubinstein understood and told me that he could make me flat, so that was why we were in his office now preparing for surgery.

I had done a lot of research about going flat after explant and even though I trusted Dr. Rubinstein, I wanted to make sure that he understood that both Wiley and I had expectations about what flat meant to us. I found several groups online that had valuable information and suggested questions to ask a surgeon.

Flat Closure Now is an advocacy group for women that educates patients and supports "going flat" as a healthy and beautiful surgical option after mastectomy. So many surgeons, male and female, have a bias against a woman choosing flat and don't even discuss it with their patients.

Another great website called *Not Putting On A Shirt* founded by Kim Bowles has a two-page flyer you can download that is easy to read and explain to surgeons. Kim was denied a satisfactory flat result after her double mastectomy and she became an advocate for satisfactory outcomes for women that choose to go flat after mastectomy.

The downloadable flyer shows photos of acceptable flat outcomes and some of the horrible photos of women that had been disrespected by their surgeons. Whether it was a result of lack of experience in making a chest flat or downright flat denial, I was not going to be denied the outcome that I deserved. Flat Denial is the term coined for waking up from surgery only to find a hot mess of skin and tissue on the front of you instead of a clean, precise flat closure.

Dr. Rubinstein looked over the two-page flyer and asked where I had gotten it. I told him all about Kim Bowles and her experience and he asked if he could keep it to share with other patients. YES! It was refreshing to find a plastic surgeon that not only listened, but was truly concerned about my mental and physical health as it related to breasts.

Dr. Rubinstein asked what my top priority was and we discussed the reality that my gorgeous cherry blossom tattoos would have to be sacrificed if in fact being flat was my top priority over saving the tattoos. I knew that I could always get my tattoos touched up, but I really did not want to have to go under the knife again if it could be avoided. I had already been through so much and I just wanted to be flat and move on with my life.

My breasts were already gone and trying to recreate something that no longer existed seemed foolish. I had already been down that road and it was far too bumpy. I wanted to get back on the smooth, flat highway and hit cruise control to enjoy the view. One and done. That is what I wanted. One more surgery and done with all of this breast garbage. Wiley and Vance wanted it too.

When I had told Wiley that I wanted to explant my breast implants and reconstruct to flat, he supported me 100%. We joked about how he would have a better rack than me, but ultimately, he told me he hadn't married me for my boobs, and he would be alright with it. After more discussion, I learned he was really an ass-man. Ha ha, the things you learn after being with someone for decades.

Dr. Rubinstein explained that he would do his best during the scheduled four-hour explant and reconstruction but a revision might be necessary. I understood that he was going to do his best to make this my last surgery and I crossed my fingers that it would be, but I also understood that needing a revision after removing all the extra skin and tissue might be necessary.

He told us to go out for a nice dinner and not to worry about getting enough sleep as I would be doing a lot of that while I healed. We took his advice and went out for a fancy steak and lobster dinner followed by a movie. I don't know why, but I always feel compelled to have a really great meal the night before surgery just in case it is my last.

The next morning, we were up with the sun and checking into the surgery center. I was the first surgery of the day and the nurses prepared me for the operating room table. I had brought a pair of socks with me that they let me wear during surgery. I couldn't resist buying the "Bye-Bye Implants" socks on Etsy. The one thing Wiley and I have always held onto in times of stress is our sense of humor. Life is so full of drama as it is, you have to make fun of even the most stressful situations. I was also glad to provide giggles to the surgery center staff. It was my thank you for the awesome care they were giving me.

Once I was all ready to go and Dr. Rubinstein had stopped in to say hello, I said my goodbyes to Wiley and we walked down the hall to the operating room. They helped me onto the operating table, spread my arms out onto the armrests positioning my arms perfectly to avoid pulling out my IV. I looked around the room at the nurses buzzing about and stared at the large operating light above my head. I don't remember anything else as the anesthesia dripped into my arm and I was out.

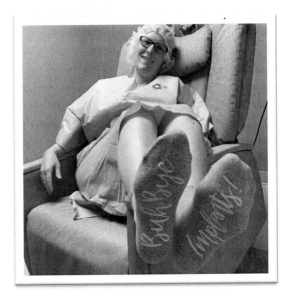

Bye-Bye Implants!

When I woke, Wiley was by my side and I was in the recovery room. I was relieved it was over and I had survived another surgery. You never know if you will be the one that had an unforeseen complication that you don't wake up from! I was groggy and out of it and needed lots of time to come around. After what seemed like hours, I was finally ready to stand up and head for the hotel.

Upon standing a wave of nausea and dizziness hit me like a ton of bricks and I almost vomited. Not quite ready yet. It took a while for me to get to the point that I was actually able to leave the facility. That was the first time I had ever experienced nausea from surgery and I went over all of the meds that had been given to me to try to figure out why I felt so sick. It didn't take long to realize it was most likely from the OxyContin® pain medication that had been given to me. I had never taken it before and in general, I don't tolerate pharmaceuticals well. I stopped the OxyContin® and switched over to the codeine that never caused me any issues and the nausea vanished. Best to stick with pharmaceuticals you know you can tolerate. Surgery isn't the best time to start experimenting with new drugs.

Dr. Rubinstein came in and told us that everything went really smoothly and that he had removed both implants along with the entire capsules En Bloc. En Bloc is the procedure of removing the implants while they are still completely covered by the tissue capsules made by my body. Removing them in this way prevents any contamination of silicone in the off chance that they were in fact ruptured and we didn't know it. Both of my implants were totally intact, thank goodness. The last thing I needed was a chest cavity full of silicone.

The nurse that had been in the operating room told us that Dr. Rubinstein had become obsessed with matching up the halves of the cherry blossoms that had been cut. He didn't want to leave my tattoos a total mess and had taken an extra hour to carefully sew them together to create whole blossoms again. He even took the time to make the scars look like the missing tree branches. I couldn't wait to see the final product, but was unable to because I was outfitted in a very tight compression garment that resembled a tube top I owned in the 1970's. I would have to wait until the unveiling at my post-op appointment the next day.

I was eager to feel better and realized that I could finally take a deep breath all the way down to the bottom of my lungs. I had been feeling short of breath before explanting due to the pressure of the implants on my ribcage and then on my lungs just underneath. The ability to take a long, deep breath was my first hint that there would be many more health benefits to come.

I have zero recollection of leaving the facility and arriving back at the hotel. I remember being cozied up under my handmade quilt and propped up by pillows while Wiley fed me yogurt with cut up banana like a baby. I slept really well that first night under the fog of anesthesia and pain pills. The following morning, Wiley and I met Dr. Rubinstein at his office bright and early. It was a Saturday and he had plans to watch his kids play soccer and we wanted to get on the road and avoid any traffic back to the desert.

Dr. Rubinstein carefully removed my bandages and revealed the new me. I was quite swollen and the incisions were red and angry, but I could tell I was on my way to being flat and finished. He laughed as he told us how he had gotten a little too into cutting and sewing my tattoos together. I was amazed at the accuracy of the matched-up blossoms considering the incisions cut right through them. My new incisions would be easily covered with new branches and blossoms in a year when I was totally healed and ready for a tattoo touch up. I was grateful and just a bit surprised at the attention to detail Dr. Rubinstein had taken while he repaired my chest after explant.

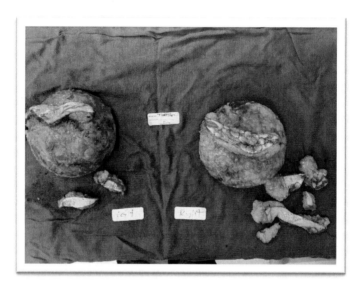

No, these are not hamburgers, they are my breast implants still encased in their scar capsule. This photo shows a true En Bloc procedure. You can see all of the extra skin, some containing my tattoos, and extra breast tissue that was removed to make me flat. Photo provided by Dr. Roee Rubinstein's office

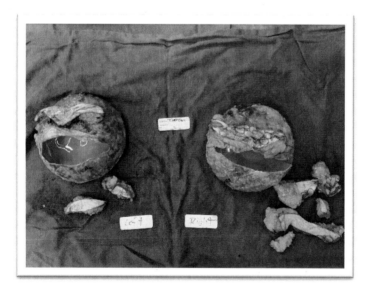

This second picture shows my scar capsules cut open to reveal the smooth, shiny silicone breast implants inside
Photo provided by Dr. Roee Rubinstein's office

Comparing the before (above photo by Ashleigh Taylor Portrait) and after (below) photos, you can see how the new scars follow the line of the original branches and the halves of blossoms were carefully sewn together to create whole blossoms. I appear to have a small breast on the right side, but it was just swelling caused by the surgery

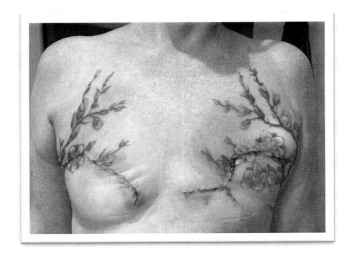

Looking at the before and after photos you are probably asking yourself how I could possibly be happy with the results, but I was very happy. It was done! I had explanted the toxic offenders and was on my way to getting my life back. I could not wait to see how my body reacted and to hopefully start losing the symptoms that had been plaguing me for two years and eight months.

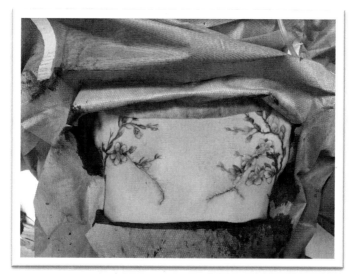

I think it is important to share the realities of surgery. This is a photo of me on the operating table after my four-hour explant. Dr. Rubinstein had finished precisely closing my incisions
Photo provided by Dr. Roee Rubinstein's office

When I look back at the time, money, pain, recovery, heartbreak, and stress that came with breast cancer, I am reminded of the old saying "You don't have anything if you don't have your health." That is an understatement and the whole reason for deconstructing my chest and returning to simply being me.

Life was starting again for me and I was so hopeful, but also annoyed that I have had to do this more than once since my cancer diagnosis. I knew that I was going to get *me* back very soon but healing from another surgery would take time. We had a long drive home and I was ready for my own bed and to start the healing process. I did not have any drains this surgery, so I would not have to make the more than four-hour drive back to see him for a whole month. I was given plastic bags filled with ice to help my swelling on the trip home. I was still very drugged from the pain medicine so I watched the green hills of Thousand Oaks turn into the sand of the California desert as the landscape passed my window and Wiley chauffeured me home. Here I come life. You don't need boobs to be beautiful!

Several weeks after explant, I received a phone call from the pathology testing facility that they were done with my breast implants and I was free to pick them up. I wasn't really sure why I wanted them, but I did, so I coordinated a day and time to drive the four hours to their facility to claim them. It was weird opening the plastic tub that contained them and a little startling to find them in bright orange biohazard bags, but not surprising. When I took them out of the tub they were so much heavier than I thought they would be, no wonder my back hurt all the time when I had them inside me. Now that I could physically hold them in my hands and I was educated about what they are made of I was amazed that I had ever agreed to letting anyone put those silicone bags inside me. It seems like such a bad idea now. I figured I would need them at some point and might want to use them as a prop at any breast implant illness events I attended, but it was just a little weird to have them back.

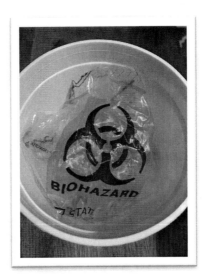

I am not a doctor and the intricacies of pathology reports are definitely not my forte so the following explanation of my results is my layman's understanding of them.

Lab testing showed both of my breast pockets had signs of foreign body reaction which is also known as chronic inflammation. Hystiocytes are a type of white blood cell and part of the immune system. They are activated by infection or inflammation and attack foreign matter in the body. Breast implants are pretty large foreign objects, so it isn't surprising that hystiocytes were present and attacking the implants.

Dr. Rubinstein had done two swabs of each breast pocket and the lab results showed no signs of anaerobic or aerobic bacteria. Anaerobic bacteria does not require oxygen to grow and aerobic bacteria does require it. Thankfully, I was negative for any bacteria.

Due to my concern about the textured implants I had for four months, both scar capsules that were removed from around the implants were tested for three different types of antibodies; CD3, CD20, and CD30. I did not have any excess fluid around either implant which was good news so only the capsules would be used for testing.

My CD3 results were positive for *Rare T-cells* but they were not anything to worry about because they were part of my immune system and play a central role in any immune response. My CD20 results were positive for a few *B-cells* but they produce antibodies necessary for fighting off infections, so not out of the ordinary for what was going on inside my body thanks to the implants. The CD30 test was the one I was most concerned about and I was incredibly relieved to find the results were *NEGATIVE* for ALCL. I honestly felt like I had dodged a bullet. My body had been clearly reacting to the implants and I had been feeling so awful and worn down all of the time because my body was putting up an immune system defense 24/7 to protect me and the lab testing confirmed it.

I noticed a huge improvement in the way I felt during the first 24 hours after explant. My brain fog disappeared and I felt clearer than I had in years. All of my joint pain and muscle soreness was gone along with the feeling that I was dying. In the weeks after explant I noticed my anxiety and panic attacks diminished and my vision seemed clearer. By the third month after explant I no longer felt chronically fatigued, I had lost six pounds, my shortness of breath was gone, and the burning pain that had surrounded my chest wall and breast implants was completely gone. The frequent urination, the swelling around my eyes, and the urinary tract infections were also completely gone and had not returned even eight months later at the time of writing this.

I felt like a completely new person. I also felt much better about my body. The breast implants made my body feel bigger and it was so good to be rid of all of it. Explant was my fourth breast surgery since being diagnosed in late 2015 and once again my body had a lot of healing to do, so I tried to take it easy and not push too hard.

Chapter Nine
How to Safely Explant

I apologize if you have breast implants and you have read all the way to this chapter because I know you are probably feeling slightly stressed by all of the information I have shared with you, it is a lot to digest, but don't panic! I have provided a list for you below based on my own experience that will help move you toward safely explanting and getting your health back. It is important that you have the explant surgery done correctly the first time or you may have to have a second surgery to go back in and remove the scar capsules. Please use the *Resources* section at the end of the book to do your homework before you take any steps toward explant as you might have other circumstances to consider before you move ahead

Explant Check List

o   Make an appointment with your primary care physician or oncologist to discuss your current symptoms and rule out any other possible medical problems that could be causing them.

o   Join the Facebook page, *Breast Implant Illness and Healing by Nicole* or go to her website; https://healingbreastimplantillness.com/ for more information and to read and share with women who know exactly what you are experiencing.

o   Lists of approved and experienced explant surgeons can be found on the websites for *Flat Closure Now*, *Not Putting on a Shirt*, and *Healing Breast Implant Illness*. Find surgeons in your area and make consultation appointments with two or three of the approved surgeons to find the one right for you.

o   Be prepared at each consultation. Print a copy of a suggested list of questions from either *Flat Closure Now*, *Not Putting on a Shirt*, or *Healing Breast Implant Illness* to interview the potential surgeons. Be sure to take notes so you can compare them later on when you are making your decision. You want to make sure that he/she will do what you ask.

o   Make sure the surgeon has experience with En Bloc or Total Capsulectomy removal of the implants. If they suggest leaving the capsule inside your body end the conversation and move onto the next surgeon. Leaving the capsule inside your body is not acceptable under any circumstances.

o   Verify with the surgeon that they will do the proper lab testing of your implants and your capsules to check for mold, fungus, bacteria, and the possibility of ALCL lymphoma.

o   If you want the implants returned to you after surgery and lab testing are completed, communicate that to the surgeon at your consultation. Some surgeons and labs refuse to return the implants to the patient even if they are intact and specifically if they are ruptured. If it is important to you, ask. They are yours, you paid for them, and I think you should be able to pick them up from the lab if that is important to you.

o   Don't be tempted to do multiple procedures at the same time as your explant. This is not the time to do a "Mommy Makeover." If you are removing implants put in for cosmetic reasons an explant and a lift is the most you want to accomplish in this surgery. Adding liposuction, a tummy tuck, or other procedures is a lot to recover from and increases your risk of serious complications.

o   If you are explanting and reconstructing to flat as a result of breast cancer, do just that. A good surgeon will want to focus on explant and getting a good flat result. Other procedures can be done separately when you are fully recovered.

o   Choose a plastic surgeon that you feel comfortable with and that listens to you. Preferably a surgeon that is no longer putting breast implants into women because it seems like a real conflict of interest to me, but it is not a requirement if the surgeon is capable and experienced. Do not let a surgeon bully you or dismiss you. If they do, get up and walk out. Breast Implant Illness is real!

o   If you are using health insurance make sure that your surgeon's office does all of the necessary paperwork to get it approved. Do not have surgery unless you have received approval or you may have to pay for the whole cost out of pocket.

o   If you are explanting implants you had for cosmetic reasons and paying out of pocket, make sure you get a quote in writing from each plastic surgeon on total cost of the procedure. Verify if there will be extra fees for the anesthesiologist, surgery center, and lab testing fees or if they are included in the quote. You don't want any financial surprises after surgery.

o   After you have chosen a surgeon, put down necessary deposits and book an explant date!

o   Make necessary arrangements for surgery including childcare, meals, and time off work to recover.

o   You've got this! If you know that explant is the best option for you, move forward. You deserve to be happy and healthy.

o   Don't let your partner, friends, or family try to convince you that your boobs are more important than your health. That is crazy! You know what is best for you and your body, don't second guess your intuition to please someone else.

o   After surgery ask for a physical therapy referral to help gain back your strength and range of motion if you need it. It is especially helpful if you are reconstructing to flat and your pectoral muscles have been repaired during explant.

- Take it easy after surgery. Do not push yourself too hard. Explanting is major surgery and your body will need time to heal and recover before you begin vigorous exercise. Ask your surgeon when it is safe to start being active and when you can resume lifting and exercising.

- Be reasonable with your expectations. While explant can relieve a lot of possible symptoms, it is not a guarantee that all of them will go away. It may take more time and patience than you would like and will depend on the length of time you had the implants along with so many other factors individual to you.

- Use the vital detox information at *Healing Breast Implant Illness* to support your body after you explant. There are foods and supplements that you might benefit from that other women have had good results with. There is also information about possible heavy metal exposure from your implants. Seek out the help of a naturopath for natural detoxing if you need the extra support.

- Spread the word! If you feel comfortable, talk about everything you have learned with your friends and family members. Be especially vocal with the young women in your family and friend's circle. You cannot suffer from breast implant illness or any of the other terrible consequences if you do not ever get implants in the first place. We need to empower young women to feel good about their bodies.

- Explant your breast implants if they are causing you problems and live your life fully! Do the things that you love and let go of any shame or blame you are feeling about choosing implants to begin with. You and millions of other women around the world made the same decision. We made a mistake. So what! We are moving on!

Chapter Ten
Understanding Informed Consent

I was ten weeks out from explant and feeling good. Better than I had in years, but I was feeling like I needed support from others going through the same experience as me. I reached out to my local cancer center and found a breast cancer information and support group to attend. Nobody understands this journey more than those that have been through it. It doesn't matter if we each had a totally different cancer and experience because we all know the fear, anger, and intense feelings that cancer invokes.

As each woman around the table introduced herself and gave a little back story, I felt so comfortable. It had been a long time since I had gone to a support group and I was happy to be in a new one in our new city. I had thought that I was totally "fine" with losing my breasts again, but it was a transition that I hadn't expected so soon after enduring reconstruction and all that entailed. I hadn't fully gotten to the point of acceptance for the silicone implants in my chest and then, just like that, they were gone.

I met about a dozen breast cancer survivors at that first meeting and knew that I was going to want to go back every week to be with them. I left the building feeling elated that I had found my support group again. What I didn't expect was the upset I experienced after a couple hours at home later that day.

When it had come to my turn to talk and introduce myself to the group, I tried as briefly as possible to explain my road to where I was today which included explant and breast implant illness. The women were all so supportive and it was definitely a safe place to share. The feelings of disappointment I experienced hours afterwards had nothing to do with the women and everything to do with the way I was feeling about my current circumstances. There were over a dozen breast cancer survivors in the group that day and most of them had not heard about explant or breast implant illness.

What I realized later is that there are cancer resource centers at very respected hospitals all across the country and the world that were not fully warning women. *How can that be? How is it considered consent if nobody is giving you the actual information that you need to make life altering decisions about your health and future?* I was upset that these amazing women didn't have all of the information about the class III medical devices implanted in their chests. Let's get real, this billion-dollar industry had been hiding its dirty little secret for decades. Breast implants can harm women and I am living proof!!!

Brochures and pamphlets on this very topic need to be given to all patients explaining the possible side effects. When I receive a prescription at the pharmacy they are required to give me a list of ingredients and all of the possible side effects to protect and inform me. This type of education and warning should also be mandatory before a medical device is implanted in the body.

I have stepped off my soapbox to clarify that I realize that breast implants are not going to go away anytime soon. There will always be a market for women's insecurities and also to help women reclaim what they have lost from breast cancer. I get it. I also believe that women should absolutely have the right to choose breast implants for cosmetic or reconstruction purposes. I am not entirely anti-implants, but after suffering as a consequence of them it is hard not to wish they were banned completely worldwide.

What I don't agree with is plastic surgeons discounting very real symptoms and health conditions that can be a side effect of any foreign object including implants placed in your body. I have endured too much on this breast cancer journey to not speak fully and freely about the realities of implants and that includes all implants; breast, pectoral, butt, chin, you name it they all can cause the same reaction in the body.

Brave women all over social media were bearing their chests, showing their scars, and describing their experiences. That was huge! I wanted to be a part of it. I wanted to make sure that there was not a single woman out there either with implants or considering them that didn't know about the risks and consequences of their decisions. If a woman decides she wants breast implants even after finding out about everything that can go wrong, I support her in her decision. She knows what is best for her and she has the information to make an informed decision.

Since my breast cancer diagnosis in November 2015, I have signed at least half a dozen *Patient Informed Consent* forms, but knowing what I know now, I don't feel like I had all the information to put my signature on those pages. I made decisions about my body, my breasts, and my future without all of the pertinent information.

Facts were hidden from me by some of my doctors but most importantly, by the FDA. Let's start by breaking down what informed consent is and what the industry already knows and should have been openly sharing with patients for decades.

As defined by the American Medical Association (AMA), *Patient Informed Consent* is the communication between the patient and the physician resulting in the patient agreeing and consenting to a specific medical intervention. Consent is based on several factors including 1) an assessment that the patient understands the relevant medical information and 2) that the physician will present the information consistent with the patient's preference for medical information. [xix]

I can tell you right now that I understood perfectly what was being explained and I had a whole list of questions about breast implants at my first plastic surgery consultation back in 2016, but the answers to my questions were downplayed and minimized.

Wiley was there with me at that first consultation and I specifically asked about the possibility that implants could cause cancer. I had read it somewhere and wanted to know what it was all about. We were told that only textured implants could cause it and that his exact words were "I don't use textured implants for that reason." I don't even remember the name of the cancer, BIA-ALCL, being discussed with us. What he said bothers me now, because months after that initial consultation my plastic surgeon put in my expanders to begin the reconstruction process. I wouldn't find out until writing this book that those expanders were actually textured and made by Allergan, the company with the most cases of ALCL. I had been told that textured were risky and so I had chosen smooth implants, but I had been put at risk without even realizing it at the time by the expanders.

Trust is so very precious between a patient and a surgeon. We trust that they will do their very best for us and protect us from harm. The AMA says that when getting informed consent from a patient, the physician should include information about 1) the diagnosis (when known), 2) the nature and purpose of the intervention and 3) the burdens, risks, and benefits including forgoing treatment.[xx]

My physician covered 1 and 2, but when it came to 3, not so much. When I asked about capsular contracture I was told that it was rare and not a problem. It was not explained to me at the time that capsular contracture actually effects between 15% - 45% of women and 92% of those cases develop within the first year.[xxi] It is the most common complaint of breast implantation! *How is that considered rare? It isn't and that is exactly what happened to me.*

I was also not informed that having my implants placed under the muscle which was the best position after my double mastectomy would entail cutting a portion of my pectoral muscles to place the implants. This can result in a loss of upper body strength and can lead to back, neck, and shoulder pain which I experienced after surgery. After I chose to remove the implants, my pectoral muscles had to be cut and repaired leading to almost four months of uncomfortable and sometimes painful physical therapy to regain my strength and range of motion. They definitely do not feel the same as they did before implants and this is as good as it gets, you cannot fully repair the pectoral muscles after being cut twice. I have noticed when I overdue it either with exercise or lifting, my pectoral muscles become very sore and I experience swelling and discomfort. I will always have to be careful with my upper body as a result of choosing under the muscle implants.

The most egregious lack of information came with no disclosure of breast implants causing autoimmune issues and autoimmune diseases. Absolutely nothing was said about this at all by anyone while I was contemplating reconstruction and it was the worst of my symptoms.

I truly wish that number 3 on the AMA's list had included a discussion about not doing any reconstruction and that choosing flat was a viable option. I had no idea that roughly 44% of women chose not to reconstruct after breast cancer. That population of women is completely invisible to the world. We are so underrepresented in the medical and oncological world and it shouldn't be surprising that going flat after my double mastectomy was never mentioned, but it should have been the first option presented.

You may be asking yourself why I didn't research all of this better or advocate for myself more enthusiastically with such an important decision. The answer is, I did, but you have to remember, I wasn't casually wandering into a plastic surgeon's office looking for a cosmetic upgrade. I was in the middle of the worst fucking nightmare of my life. I had a very aggressive, stage 2 breast cancer that needed to come out and I needed to make decisions quickly.

Breast cancer patients are pushed forward at lightning speed when what we really should be offered is more time. Time to heal, time to sit with our choices, time to contemplate the best decision for our long-term health. Time to read and educate ourselves. Everyone in the oncology field should be handing out information with a list of the real pros and cons associated with each and every procedure offered.

Breast implants are not life time devices and this was told to me at my consultation. I knew that every eight to ten years I would need to replace my implants. I figured I would have at least one set, maybe two, and then I would be in my sixties and would just go flat. I didn't even make it three full years with implants. Had I been given all of the information known to date about breast implants, I might have made a different decision. I certainly would have been better prepared for the side effects I experienced that went largely ignored until I was desperately sick.

As a result of women testifying to the FDA, filing adverse reaction reports, and writing letters on the topic of breast implants the FDA is finally taking steps to protect women. They are working on updating informed consent forms that will cover ALCL and autoimmune diseases. There is current discussion about a possible black box warning for all breast implants. The biggest change so far has been a total ban of textured implants in the US and across the globe that was announced in July 2019. This is definite progress, but until women have all of the information we have to keep speaking up and educating.

Chapter Eleven
The True Cost of Breast Implants

What is the real cost of breast implants? I can tell you from personal experience that it is much more than you think and it isn't just monetary. For women choosing implants for cosmetic reasons, insurance does not currently cover any of the cost so these figures will all be out of pocket. For women doing reconstruction with implants as a result of breast cancer, insurance will pay the majority of the surgery but there will be out of pocket costs including; copays, surgery costs, lab testing fees, physical therapy copays, travel expenses, time off work, and more.

1.) The average cost of a new set of breast implants for cosmetic reasons in the US is between $5,000-$10,000 depending on location and doctor. [xxii]

2.) Every 8-10 years you will need to have them replaced. They are NOT lifetime devices.[xxiii] As a result, you will need to deduct another $5,000-$10,000 from your bank account every decade for replacement. If you develop capsular contracture which is estimated to affect between 15-45% of women[xxiv], you may need to replace the implants sooner than 8-10 years.

3.) If your breast implants rupture they will have to be replaced because you do not want the contents to leak into your body. Saline implants can be filled with mold and other harmful bacteria that can grow in your chest cavity. Silicone spilling into your body can cause a myriad of health problems including the possibility of Silicone toxicity. Ruptures are more common the older the implants. Saline implants deflate when ruptured so you will want them replaced or removed so you don't have to live with one breast smaller than the other. Depending on the warranty for your implants, you may be able to get the manufacturer to give you a new set of replacement implants if they spontaneously rupture but you will be responsible for surgery costs. More $$$ and more surgery to fix them.

4.) If you suffer from BII (breast implant illness) symptoms you will most likely search out doctors and health practitioners in an attempt to find relief from the illness. Heavy metal testing, blood tests, autoimmune disease testing (ANA panel), visits to cardiologists, rheumatologists, oncologists, naturopaths, vitamins, minerals, detoxification programs... you get the picture. A lot more $$$ for complimentary therapies that will not fix the problem, but will empty your bank account while you continue to suffer.

5.) If you acquire an autoimmune disease as a result of your implants you could be adding a lifetime of medical costs to treat the disease. Worse yet, if you contract one of the known breast implant associated cancers like BIA-ALCL, you will need explant surgery, lab testing, the possibility of chemotherapy, and if the lymphoma has spread, you are at risk of death as a result of your implants.

6.) If you change your mind and decide that you would like to remove the implants, you will need to find a board-certified plastic surgeon with experience in removing the implants along with the scar capsule in a procedure called En bloc or Total Capsulectomy. Your body created the scar capsule around the implant to protect you from the foreign object and it must come out with the implant to protect you from future problems. Explant costs vary widely, but you are looking at about $5,000-$30,000 depending on location and doctor without insurance. Some women have been successful in getting their medical insurance to cover some of the costs but at this time that is not guaranteed.

7.) If your implants were put in for cosmetic reasons you will most likely need to include a breast lift with your explant to restore the shape of your breasts. The weight of breast implants stretches your skin and when removed a lift will remove excess baggy skin. A lift will add thousands of dollars to your procedure and more scars and healing time.

8.) If your implants are sub-pectoral (under the muscle) it is possible that your surgeon will need to cut and repair your pectoral muscles during your explant surgery to restore them. This can add more discomfort during recovery and the need for physical therapy. Physical therapy can help you regain your range of motion and improve recovery of your pectoral muscles. The average cost of PT without insurance is between $75-$150 each session. I hope you have planted a money tree at this point, because you are going to need it in full bloom if you have any problems with your implants.

9.) All of this talk about money has ignored the pain and suffering that accompanies any surgery. You will have to take time off of work and so will your partner or a friend to help care for you during recovery. The more complications you have the more complicated the surgery can become.

10.) Cutting your breasts open and sewing them closed multiple times can create scar tissue that is not only unsightly but painful and in need of further treatment. Keloid scarring or hypertrophic scarring can thicken scars and create problems. I developed hypertrophic scarring after the first round of surgeries to put in my implants. After explant it developed again. Both times my scarring issues required months of uncomfortable cortisone shots directly into my breast scars from a dermatologist. More pain and money as a result of my implants. There are so many unknowns when choosing breast implants. You cannot plan exactly how your body will react in the days, weeks, months and even years after they are placed.

11.) Set aside the monetary cost of breast implants. The biggest possible cost of implants is your physical and mental health. Mahatma Gandhi famously said, "Your health is your real wealth." This cannot be understated. What is the true cost of breast implants? Peace of mind, self-esteem, confidence, self-worth, time with your friends and family, self-loathing, your sanity, feelings of shame, and so many more unsettling issues. Some of those issues are the exact reasons why you chose to put implants in your chest in the first place. I wish breast implants could fix all of our insecurities but they don't and in some cases, they amplify them.

You may think that I am trying to scare you out of choosing implants and in a way, I am. I don't want you or someone you love to have to go through all of the possible complications that hundreds of thousands of women are now experiencing and complaining about. These are not just scare tactics, they are the facts. The facts that I didn't know when I made the choice.

If you log onto the internet there is so much more information about breast implants now that may pertain to your situation that I haven't even touched upon here. We each have our own genetic issues and there is no way to know how you will react once you implant these foreign objects in your body.

If you still want a set of breast implants after everything you have read here, I truly wish you the best. I hope that you have all of the information needed to make an informed decision about your future health.

Before you book that surgery date, write that deposit check, or whip out that credit card, take a look down the road. In five to ten years will you have enough money to replace or remove your implants? What will your partner think about you removing them? How will you explain it to your children? There are so many things to think about before you permanently change your breasts and they will be changed forever.

The money you spend today may be just the beginning of a very expensive and uncomfortable journey. Before you pay the surgeon's deposit, talk to a therapist about the reasons you are wanting breast implants for cosmetic reasons in the first place. The average therapist runs between $60-$120 per session and you could be saving yourself tens of thousands of dollars by getting to the bottom of why you feel that the breasts you have are not acceptable. This decision is bigger than you can possibly imagine and I wish I would have talked this through with a professional before I chose it.

Yes, I had breast cancer and was left deformed after a total double mastectomy. Breast implants were a perfectly natural response to that loss. I wish I had known what I know now about these class III medical devices. Their implantation and removal is far more complicated and damaging than I was told. If you are injured by your implants or any other class III medical device, in the majority of cases you have no legal recourse to sue the manufacturer. They are protected by the law of preemption.

The law of preemption states that Federal law is superior to state law. States cannot impose requirements that go against state law. Medical devices are regulated by the FDA and are therefore considered preempted. FDA official Randall Lutter told Congress, "FDA believes that the important decisions it makes about the safety, efficacy and labeling of medical products should not be second guessed by state courts." [xxv]

The FDA has not only admitted to hiding millions of adverse reports against class III medical devices, they have made it easier for the manufacturers to get them approved. Watch the Netflix documentary, *The Bleeding Edge*, and you will be stunned at the process of rushing new medical devices through approval without proper clinical trials. We are the guinea pigs in this billion-dollar medical device industry with no recourse if they cause us illness, disfigure our bodies, or even kill us. Getting a new set of boobs doesn't seem like a big deal but the truth is they come with a whole slew of very serious possible consequences. Buyer Beware!

Chapter Twelve
FLAT is Where it's At

Three months after explanting to flat I was invited to be a guest on *The Doctors* television show with over a dozen other breast implant illness survivors. I was excited to find out that my BII sister, Talia Krainock Maddock, that had helped me so much during our phone call in the beginning of this journey would be flying in from Texas for the taping. I would finally get to meet her in person.

Eden Sassoon, the daughter of Vidal Sassoon and former *Beverly Hills Housewife* would be sharing her story along with Angie Everhart, actress and former *Sports Illustrated* model. Talia, Eden, and Angie would be front and center on stage to share their experiences with breast implant illness. My friend and breast cancer survivor, Sunshine, that had introduced me to BII and Talia, joined us that day to lend support. Sunshine and I arrived at the Paramount Pictures Studio lot on a sunny California morning in late August 2019 for the taping. We joined all of the women on the set of *Dr. Phil* while we waited to be called to *The Doctors* set for taping. We shared our stories while we waited and I discovered that I was the only breast cancer survivor participating and the only flat woman that would be on the stage that day, everyone else had chosen breast implants for cosmetic reasons.

Once we were all situated on the stage, the high energy music of Beyoncé's *Run the World (Girls)* song blasted through the speakers and the regular weekly cast of the doctors joined us onstage as we clapped and danced as they entered. The doctors included; Dr. Travis Stork, the show's host, plastic surgeon; Dr. Andrew (Drew) P. Ordon, and Clinical and Forensic Psychologist; Dr. Judy Ho. They were joined by special guests; Dr. Kristi Funk author of *Breasts the Owner's Manual* and recommended explant plastic surgeon Dr. Ritu Chopra.

Sunshine and I taking a selfie on the Paramount Studios lot
with the iconic water tower landmark in the background
Photo taken by Kathleen (Sunshine) O' Brien

We were asked to bring our actual breast implants to hold up for an episode
promo we would tape with host Dr. Travis Stork. After handling the implants
for over an hour out of their biohazard bag, my hands became very itchy causing
me to believe that I was definitely still sensitive to silicone. Several other
women in the group said the same thing was happening to their hands.
Photo taken by Kathleen (Sunshine) O' Brien

Even though the majority of us didn't get the time to share our
individual stories, we were there to support bringing the truth about
breast implant illness to the masses. Every chair on the stage was
filled with a woman that had experienced the side effects of a class
III medical device that the FDA had said was safe but had made us
all sick. The consequences of our decisions to put them in our
chests could no longer be ignored. I imagined women across the
globe watching and finding out that the mysterious symptoms they
had been experiencing were quite possibly caused by their implants

and they never would have known if *The Doctors* hadn't decided to do an episode on BII. I made some wonderful connections that day and loved being on a television set.

About five months after the taping, I received a message from a woman on Instagram that told me she had never heard of BII until she watched that episode. She had her ruptured thirty-year old Dow Corning implants removed in 2012 in a twenty-minute surgery, so clearly her scar capsules were not removed with them. She thanked me for sharing the information because she was still very sick and had no answers until now. She was seeing a specialist and having tests done because of that information. It really is true that reaching even just one person makes it all worthwhile and we reached her.

Being involved in the taping of that episode and owning my flat chest that day on a television show that would be seen by millions worldwide was very empowering for me. It pushed me further to get involved in becoming a flat advocate and motivated me to continue to speak about breast cancer, reconstruction, implants, and everything that comes along with a breast cancer diagnosis.

I was still getting used to my new flat reality and reluctant to show my bare chest to anyone not in my immediate family and friends circle. I was presenting myself as flat in my day to day life because I no longer had breasts and therefore didn't need a bra anymore. I always hated wearing bras, so not having to wear one was liberating. On occasion, I would wear a bralette with padding if my outfit dictated but I really felt much more comfortable just being me.

It was October 2018 and the scourge of pink ribbons was upon us again. In the beginning of my diagnosis I thought the whole pink ribbon movement was awesome, but as the months and years went by I started to see the ugly truth of it all. I had become aware of the term *pink-washing* which describes the overuse of pink ribbons to sell products. Corporations slapped a pink ribbon on their products to increase sales and brand loyalty and in return they promised to donate small amounts of money to the cause. A lot of the products donning a pink ribbon in support of breast cancer actually contain chemicals known to cause all kinds of cancers. It is all very nauseating, but I wanted to do something for *Breast Cancer Awareness Month*, but something that mattered. I signed up for a breast cancer fundraising walk in Palm Desert that would benefit the Desert Cancer Foundation. All of the money raised would be staying in the Coachella Valley and helping cancer patients financially. My breast cancer support group would be walking in it and I was really looking forward to the group activity.

I had become aware of a community of women on Facebook that had organized their first weekend *Flat Retreat* in Palm Springs. The women were traveling from all over the US and Canada to spend the weekend together and they would be at the walk too. I was unable to attend the retreat, but joined their online group and hoped to attend future flat positive events.

The day of the walk I met up with all of the amazing women in my local breast cancer support group. We were all wearing our pink shirts and hats and ready to walk to raise money to support those going through cancer in our valley. We had all been there and knew the true cost of a cancer diagnosis both physically and financially.

The walk was set up in a loop from one end of El Paseo street to the other. As we walked toward the mountains, a group of women walking in the opposite direction caught my eye. They were loud, arm in arm, and TOPLESS! I had never seen anything like it! They were all FLAT and had removed their shirts to show the world what it looked like to be flat; no nipples, no breasts, lots of scars, and all courage! One of the woman walking with me vocalized that she was torn about the display and feared that it would scare woman newly diagnosed. My other friends, Donna and Carla thought it was empowering. I thought it was badass and totally inspirational, but I also told them that I was definitely not ready for that level of personal exposure. Funny because my last book was a *Vulnerable Photographic Journey* of my breasts for all to see.

After completing the walk and saying goodbye to my friends, I walked down El Paseo toward my car. El Paseo Shopping District is in the center of Palm Desert and a hub for restaurants and shops. I was looking at my phone and not really paying much attention to the women around me until I looked up and saw the topless group coming toward me. Their *Flat Retreat* shirts were tucked into the front of their shorts and that is when I realized who they were. I had to meet them!

I walked up and introduced myself to their fearless leader, Stacey Sigman, whom I had met online. She gave me a huge hug when she recognized me and the other women asked if I was also flat. "YES! I am a FLATTIE!" I proudly exclaimed as they cheered me on. They asked me if I wanted to take off my shirt and join them. Ten minutes earlier I had said out loud to several breast cancer survivors that I was not at all ready for bearing my chest in public, but here I was surrounded by a group of fiercely flat women, so I didn't even hesitate. I later found out that they had originally planned to go shirtless to raise awareness, but then they had all collectively decided that they were not ready to expose themselves publicly. In the moment, they changed their minds and their act of courage inspired myself and thousands of other participants that day at the walk.

I removed my pink cancer t-shirt and walked forward arm in arm with a group of women I didn't even know. It was the most amazing moment! I was free! I was letting go of the last remaining remnants of my fear of being flat and embracing it with a tribe of women I instantly felt bonded with. Sometimes pushing yourself out of your comfort zone is what you need to do to move forward and build self-confidence.

Breast cancer is scary! There is no way to go through it without being terrified. Our cancer scars are beautiful and it is ok to be proud of them. If anyone was scared that day seeing our scars we were not aware of it. We were openly cheered on by men and women that saw how brave the act of bearing the real-life consequences of breast cancer can be. The news media outlets interviewed the *Flat Retreat* ladies and dozens of women approached the group thanking them for their bravery.

It was not an easy journey to flat and I wish no other woman would ever have to go through this, but every year in the US alone, over 300,000 women and a small percentage of men will be diagnosed with some type of breast cancer.[xxvi] I want every single one of those women to have all of the information they need to choose what their chest will look like. Choosing to be flat and unreconstructed is a valid, healthy, and beautiful choice and in most cases no further surgery is needed.

Six months after my explant surgery I was bothered by a pretty good size lump on my left side above my armpit. Dr. Rubinstein and I had hoped that it would resolve itself after I was fully healed but it didn't. I could have tried to live with it but every time I moved my arm I felt a pulling inside that went up to my shoulder. It wasn't painful, just uncomfortable and I asked Dr. Rubinstein to remove it surgically. He had warned me that revision surgery may be necessary after the explant and reconstruction and in my case, it was. I had the revision surgery and the lump was removed very quickly and with no complications. It turned out to be extra skin and subcutaneous fat that was a result of my original expansion. I was happy to find that the discomfort resolved as a result too. I was glad I didn't try to live with it and got it taken care of. Six surgeries in three years is too many but now I was truly done.

If you choose to reconstruct with breast implants you may be one of the lucky ones that don't complain about any symptoms. You also need to know that your health could be fine for years with no apparent problems, but at some point, you could start to have issues as the silicone and heavy metals bleed into your body through the shell of the implant. Your immune system will be fighting the foreign objects in your body 24/7 for as long as you have them and like me, you won't realize that they are a problem as the symptoms slowly accumulate over the years to the point that you cannot ignore them. *Will it be worth it?* That is a question that only you can answer, but I can tell you from personal experience that I wish I could go back in time and tell my original plastic surgeon that I wanted to be FLAT! I would have spent the last four years fully living instead of barely surviving.

In 1998 Congress passed the *Women's Health and Cancer Rights Act (WHCRA)* which mandated health insurance companies pay for breast reconstruction after a woman undergoes a single or double mastectomy due to cancer.[xxvii] The law was sound, but according to *Flat Closure Now* it had unintentional consequences for women who did not want to reconstruct. The prevailing belief among plastic surgeons is that women in general would be happier with breasts than without. Women are pressured into reconstruction, especially those that are younger and I definitely felt that after my mastectomy. Sadly, even if a woman has chosen not to reconstruct, in many cases she is denied an acceptable flat closure by her surgeon.[xxviii]

I have had women show me their mangled chests on more than one occasion and it is so upsetting. These women specifically asked to be flat and the surgeons left them with enough skin and/or tissue to reconstruct, just in case they changed their minds. In some cases, the surgeon lacked the skills to provide an adequate flat closure, but had promised it. This attitude is paternalistic and unacceptable.

It presumes that a woman can't make the decision about how she wants to look after surviving breast cancer. It is an attitude that *doctor knows best* which is completely false and ignores the fact that choosing flat is empowering for the survivor and we still feel whole even without breasts.

Flat Closure NOW and *Not Putting on a Shirt* are two organizations that have many resources for women contemplating going flat, including finding a surgeon and surgical questions. Both non-profit groups are dedicated to working with health care providers to develop clear language that leaves no question about what a woman means when she says she wants to *"go flat."* I highly recommend starting your flat journey by visiting both of their websites and/or Facebook pages.

Stefanie Swafford Gibson and I showing off our chest tattoos in public at the Paint El Paseo Pink breast cancer awareness walk benefitting the Desert Cancer Foundation. Photo by Diane Loewen

Four very supportive California Highway Patrol officers joined my new flat tribe for a photo at the Paint El Paseo Pink breast cancer awareness event in Palm Desert. Front, Left to right: Lupe Marie Guillen, Gina Kohn, Elizabeth Dale, LA Mitchell, Stefanie Swafford Gibson, Joy Smith, Dara Dunbar, Holly K. Thrasher, Teri Kincaid, Linda Pruden, and Carol Contos-Cursi.
Photo by Diane Loewen

All of these experiences since becoming flat have had a profound effect on me and how I feel about my body. For the first time in my life I have been able to replace that little voice in my head with an outspoken, supportive, kick-ass voice that says I am worthy without breasts and that my life is worth far more alive than dead. I will continue to keep stepping up and speaking out, because I have found my voice and I know there are others that need to hear it. It's going to be hard to shut me up now!

Living with a flat chest is definitely different than living with breasts, but it, like most things, is what YOU make of it. There are many bras and prosthetic options available, some covered by insurance that can be used to give the appearance of breasts if you feel more comfortable with them.

I have found that ruffles, patterns, off the shoulder shirts, and certain styles of dresses actually camouflage my flatness and provide me the confidence to be out in the world without breasts. I cannot stress enough, boobs alone do not make you sexy or a woman!

Our society oversexualizes women's bodies and breasts to the point of absurdity. It is a way to keep us down, enslaved to the notion that we are here to please men. We are not! We are independent, autonomous, and extremely brave every day in the face of a culture that shames our bodies and silences our voices. Part of my flat journey has been fighting against those ideas and promoting the idea that my body is mine alone and I do not owe anyone anything when it comes to how I dress or if I have boobs or not. Being a flattie has ignited my inner rebellion and I am owning it! It may also be a result of being in my fifties and finally deciding to embrace myself fully, body and mind.

I want to also vocalize my continued support for those breast cancer survivors that do choose to reconstruct. I understand and sympathize with the desire to have breasts, it is the reason why I originally chose reconstruction with implants. If my body hadn't rejected them I would still be living with them and probably very happy. I have many friends living with breast implants as a result of cancer and others for cosmetic reasons. I want to let you all know that I support your decision either way. I am here for you in either circumstance.

I do not want any other woman to suffer like I did and I am not the only one. There are over a hundred thousand women online in the breast implant illness Facebook group talking about their experiences too. There needs to be long-term extensive clinical studies done on breast implants and what happens to them when they are inside our bodies. The implant manufacturers have gotten away with minimal research and we are essentially guinea pigs with no ability to sue if things go wrong. The law of preemption needs to change to protect the millions of consumers being implanted with class III medical devices in the US.

As a breast cancer survivor, the reality of the inevitability of death is hard to ignore. It is with us every waking moment and we have to work hard to not let it overshadow everything else in our lives. I have endured many days feeling down and less-than I was before cancer, but choosing to become flat after such a bad experience with implants has been empowering for me and an important step in claiming my body back. It has also helped me overcome the PTSD type anxiety that was introduced into my mind and body after diagnosis and treatment. I know that not every woman wanting breast implants will get to this same place emotionally, but I wish they could. I am going to say it again, boobs don't make you a woman and you can live a full life and be sexy without them!

I think we need to change the narrative surrounding breast cancer and reconstruction. The prevailing idea that breast cancer awareness is all about saving our breasts is wrong. This is not about our breasts! This is about saving our lives! We need to come together as a collective and push for breast cancer research to find a cure. *"Saving the Tatas"* continues the false narrative that breasts make women whole after breast cancer. Too many of us our dying and looking at the bigger picture, saving our breasts is the least important aspect of this disease. Every minute a woman dies of breast cancer somewhere in the world. That's more than 1,400 women every single day leaving their families because their cancer couldn't be cured.[xxix] We have to change those numbers. Finding a cure for breast cancer should be the primary focus and it cannot start soon enough.

I love being flat and not just because the alternative was to be dead. Honestly, I am alive and that should be enough. I look in the mirror and tell myself that I am enough. I am beautiful without breasts. I am sorry that I put my body through the breast implants, the cancer was traumatic enough. Like every other human being on the planet, I have insecurities, but I am now choosing to live everyday with the life I have been given and the body that I have. This reframing of my own perceptions about my body is truly a gift and so is my health. I hope you choose your health over your vanity, it has been a tough lesson for me to learn, but one of the most valuable.

Now, please go and spread the word about breast implants far and wide. We need to make sure that the next generation of young women understand the risks and choose not to implant them for cosmetic reasons. Body positivity and body acceptance no matter what shape or size we are should be the focus, not the size of our breasts.

It is time that the FDA and all of us hold the breast implant manufacturers accountable for the side effects, cancers, and deaths that their products have caused. We need to force the manufacturers to do adequate safety studies that the FDA originally required when they allowed implants back on the market in early 2000's, but never enforced. This industry is in business with our money and until they prove that implants are safe with clinical research, I think that we should stop giving it to them! We have all the power and we need to start using it. My Mother used to say, "You vote with your dollars." She couldn't be more right and I choose to vote NO when it comes to breast implants until they are proven to be a safe class III medical device. I hope you will join me in speaking out and pressuring the powerful to do the right thing.

My all-time favorite photo of my biggest supporter and the love of my life,
Wiley Dean Thrasher. Photo by the talented Ashleigh Taylor Portrait

Resources

The following resources will help you find further information and qualified medical professionals. There are so many more than listed here, but these are the resources I personally used. I have found communities of women on Facebook that support, educate, and empower, so I highly recommend joining one or more listed below. Our voices are stronger when we join them together. I am not a paid endorser of any of the resources listed.

Facebook Private Groups for Breast Implant Illness Support:
- Breast Implant Illness and Healing by Nicole
- California Healing Breast Implant Illness
- Itty Bitty Breast Implant Illness Support
- Breast Implant Lawsuits
- ALCL in Women with Breast Implants BIA-ALCL
- Dr. Rubinstein Breast Explant Patient Support Group

Facebook Private Groups for Flat Support:
- Fabulously Flat (Unreconstructed Breast Cancer Survivors)
- Fierce, Flat, Forward
- Flatties Unite: Flat Closure Community & Support
- Warrior Flatties
- Flat & Fabulous

Facebook Groups for Breast Cancer Support:
- Desert Cancer Foundation
- Shay's Warriors

Facebook Pages for Information:
- Holly K Thrasher
- Flat Closure NOW
- Breast Implant Safety Alliance
- Flat Retreat
- Not Putting On A Shirt
- Alliance for Breast Implant Education (ABIE)
- Shay's Warriors – Life After Cancer

Informational Webpages:
- Healing Breast Implant Illness
  healingbreastimplantillness.com
- Flat Closure Now
  flatclosurenow.org
- Breast Implant Safety Alliance
  Breastimplantsafetyalliance.org
- Not Putting on a Shirt
  Notputtingonashirt.org
- Alliance for Breast Implant Education (ABIE)
  Abie.life
- Shay's Warriors – Life After Cancer
  ShaysWarriors.org
- Desert Cancer Foundation
  Desert Cancer Foundation.org

Informational Podcasts:
- *Let's Talk Breast Health*, Host: Talia Krainock Maddock, Listen at: The LIVE Broadcast Network on Facebook or Letstalkbreasthealth.com

- *On Air with Angie Everhart*, Host: Angie Everhart, Listen at: On Air with Angie Everhart on Facebook.

Acknowledgements

Thank you to everyone that has supported me on my journey through breast cancer, BII, and becoming a published author. Especially those mentioned here. I couldn't have done it without you! I am deeply grateful for the assistance, encouragement, and superior care of Dr. Roee Rubinstein and Dr. Robert R. Jordan. Melissa Flores at Dynamic Physical Therapy helped me regain use of my pectoral muscles after explant surgery. Thank you to the BII community who are getting the word out; Nicole Daruda, Christie Avila, Julie Lykins, Jane Rimer, Robyn Towt, Tara Hopko, Angie Everhart, Eden Sassoon, Talia Krainock Maddock, Kathleen (Sunshine) O'Brien, and all of the activists committed to speaking out for all BII survivors. Thank you, Flat Retreat for letting me join your Tribe; Stacey Sigman, Diane Loewen, Lupe Marie Guillen, Gina Kohn, Elizabeth Dale, Linda Pruden, Stefanie Swafford Gibson, Joy Smith, Dara Dunbar, Teri Kincaid, LA Mitchell, Carol Contos-Cursi, Sheila Pemstein, Samantha Wellman, and all of the other ladies in attendance that were so supportive. So much love and respect to my local breast cancer support group who share, listen, and support each other every day; Anji Aguas, Carla Teran, Diane Delatorre, Donna Larson, Elaine Childs, Gloria Luces, Joan Sorensen, Margie Tinsley, Mona-Lisa Smith, Patrice Coffee, Rebekah Dickerson-Roberson, Rose Levy, Samantha Marji, Shay Moraga, Vicki Plavchak, and all of the women that have the courage to continually show up to the group to help other cancer survivors. I will always cherish my cherry blossom tattoos and original artwork from Sebastian Orth at Otherworld Tattoo. Ashleigh Taylor, Wiley and I love the photos you took of us, thank you for allowing me to share them with the world. One of the best things in life is having a best friend that is always there to support you... Thank you Rosalie Zabilla. A lifetime of thanks to my amazing family members; June, Ken, Lauren, Brandon, Riley, Sarah, Donald, Madison, Austin, Susie, Bill, Carolynne, Dixon, and Karen for continually having to hear about my boobs and being so supportive about it! I promise the next book won't be about my cancer or breasts. I am lucky to wake up every day with my best friend, Wiley, who keeps me laughing and never gives up on me. One of the best gifts in my life is our son, Vance, thank you for your impeccable copy-editing skills on both of my books. I love you all!

Also by Holly K. Thrasher

Bittersweet: A Vulnerable Photographic Breast Cancer Journey

Bittersweet original cover art by Vera Long

"Rarely does one show others the vulnerability of a healing transformation as Holly has in Bittersweet. Highly informative as well as raw, powerful, and courageous, women (and their families) will find within these pages a true friend and guide during their own healing journey and hopefully will know their path can lead to greater beauty, strength and fortitude in the process. Inspiring, at times harrowing, and even funny, I believe readers everywhere will become more empowered by reading these pages."
- Zhena Muzyka, Author, Life by the Cup
& Women's Empowerment Advocate

"I am so impressed with Holly's willingness to share her story with the goal of bringing awareness to our collective cancer journey in such a beautiful way. She will always be an inspiration to me, as I watched her go from diagnosis to thriver with the most positive attitude I have seen."
- Susan Kapadia, Founder & Executive Director, OjaiCARES

"Holly has done something extraordinary with this book - she has demystified the phases of the breast cancer journey in a most soulful, intimate and courageous way. Bittersweet is not only an invaluable source of information but also a means of empowerment and enlightenment for anyone with this diagnosis."
- Pamela Robins, Author, Meditating with Animals

Continuing the Story
Engage with Holly at:

HollyKThrasher.com

Facebook: HollyKThrasher

Instagram: @HollyKThrasher

Twitter: @HollyKThrasher

Youtube: HollyKThrasher

Notes

Endnotes

[i] Wilkins EG, Hamill JB, Kim HM, et al. *Complications in Post Mastectomy Breast Reconstruction: One-year Outcomes of the Mastectomy Reconstruction Outcomes Consortium* (MROC) Study. *Ann Surg.* 2018;267(1):164–170. doi:10.1097/SLA.0000000000002033
https://www.ncbi.nlm.nih.gov/pmc/articles/PMC5904787/

[ii] Wilkins EG, Hamill JB, Kim HM, et al. *Complications in Post Mastectomy Breast Reconstruction: One-year Outcomes of the Mastectomy Reconstruction Outcomes Consortium* (MROC) Study. *Ann Surg.* 2018;267(1):164–170. doi:10.1097/SLA.0000000000002033
https://www.ncbi.nlm.nih.gov/pmc/articles/PMC5904787/

[iii] Wilkins EG, Hamill JB, Kim HM, et al. *Complications in Post Mastectomy Breast Reconstruction: One-year Outcomes of the Mastectomy Reconstruction Outcomes Consortium* (MROC) Study. *Ann Surg.* 2018;267(1):164–170. doi:10.1097/SLA.0000000000002033
https://www.ncbi.nlm.nih.gov/pmc/articles/PMC5904787/

[iv] *FDA Risks and Complications of Breast Implants*,
https://www.fda.gov/medical-devices/breast-implants/risks-and-complications-breast-implants

[v] Healing Breast Implant Illness, *Breast Implant Safety* ,
https://healingbreastimplantillness.com/breast-implant-safety/

[vi] Healing Breast Implant Illness, *Breast Implant Illness and Silicone Toxicity Symptoms*, https://healingbreastimplantillness.com/breast-implant-illness-symptoms/

[vii] Healing Breast Implant Illness by Nicole Daruda, *Breast Implant Illness Symptoms*, https://healingbreastimplantillness.com/breast-implant-illness-symptoms/

[viii] American Society of Plastic Surgeons, *What is capsular contracture and how can it be treated?* Kevin Tehrani, MD, New York, NY, June 12, 2018. https://www.plasticsurgery.org/news/blog/what-is-capsular-contracture-and-how-can-it-be-treated

[ix] Mayo Clinic, *ANA Test Overview*
https://www.mayoclinic.org/tests-procedures/ana-test/about/pac-20385204

[x] Allergan, Inc. brochure "*Finding the right fit. A Guide to Breast Augmentation with the Natrelle Collection*," The safety of silicone, page 3, 2007

[xi] Jury Faults Dow Chemical in Breast-Implant Trial, The Washington Post, by John Schwarz, August 19,1997, https://www.washingtonpost.com/archive/politics/1997/08/19/jury-faults-dow-chemical-in-breast-implant-trial/e143158e-d23b-4b77-80de-a7e319f3f456/

[xii] *FDA Backgrounder on Platinum in Silicone Breast Implants*, https://www.fda.gov/medical-devices/breast-implants/fda-backgrounder-platinum-silicone-breast-implants

[xiii] Healing Breast Implant Illness by Nicole Daruda, *Breast Implant Safety* https://healingbreastimplantillness.com/breast-implant-safety/

[xiv] Allergan, Inc. brochure *"Finding the right fit. A Guide to Breast Augmentation with the Natrelle Collection,"* The history of silicone gel-filled breast implants, page 3, 2007.

[xv] Allergan, Inc. brochure *"Finding the right fit. A Guide to Breast Augmentation with the Natrelle Collection,"* The history of silicone gel-filled breast implants, page 4, 2007.

[xvi] Abdulla Watad et al. *Silicone breast implants and the risk of autoimmune/rheumatic disorders: a real-world analysis*, International Journal of Epidemiology (2018). DOI: 10.1093/ije/dyy217 https://medicalxpress.com/news/2018-11-silicone-breast-implant-patients-greatly.html

[xvii] Abdulla Watad et al. *Silicone breast implants and the risk of autoimmune/rheumatic disorders: a real-world analysis*, International Journal of Epidemiology (2018). DOI: 10.1093/ije/dyy217 https://medicalxpress.com/news/2018-11-silicone-breast-implant-patients-greatly.html

[xviii] *"FDA to end program that hid millions of reports on faulty medical devices,"* May 5, 2019, by Christina Jewett, Kaiser Health News. https://www.pbs.org/newshour/health/fda-to-end-program-that-hid-millions-of-reports-on-faulty-medical-devices

[xix] American Medical Association, *Code of Ethics, Informed Consent.* https://www.ama-assn.org/delivering-care/ethics/informed-consent

[xx] American Medical Association, *Code of Ethics, Informed Consent.* https://www.ama-assn.org/delivering-care/ethics/informed-consent

[xxi] *Incidence of capsular contracture in silicone versus saline cosmetic augmentation mammoplasty: A meta-analysis.* El-Sheikh Y, Tutino R, Knight C, Farrokhyar F, Hynes N. *Can J Plast Surg.* 2008;16(4):211–215. doi:10.1177/229255030801600403 https://www.ncbi.nlm.nih.gov/pmc/articles/PMC2691025/

[xxii] WebMD, *Breast Implants*, https://www.webmd.com/beauty/cosmetic-procedures-breast-augmentation#1

[xxiii] US Federal Drug Administration (FDA), *Risks and Complications of Breast Implants*, https://www.fda.gov/medical-devices/breast-implants/risks-and-complications-breast-implants

[xxiv] *Incidence of capsular contracture in silicone versus saline cosmetic augmentation mammoplasty: A meta-analysis.* El-Sheikh Y, Tutino R, Knight C, Farrokhyar F, Hynes N. *Can J Plast Surg.* 2008;16(4):211–215. doi:10.1177/229255030801600403 https://www.ncbi.nlm.nih.gov/pmc/articles/PMC2691025/

[xxv] *Preemption*, Elaine Silvestrini, May 16, 2019, https://www.drugwatch.com/lawsuits/preemption/

[xxvi] Breastcancer.org, *Symptoms* https://www.breastcancer.org/symptoms/understand_bc/statistics

[xxvii] Centers for Medicare and Medicaid Services, *The Center for Consumer Information & Insurance Oversight*, CMS.gov https://www.cms.gov/CCIIO/Programs-and-Initiatives/Other-Insurance-Protections/whcra_factsheet

[xxviii] Flat Closure Now, *About*, https://www.flatclosurenow.org/about

[xxix] Susan G. Komen, Breast Cancer Fact Sheet, 2018 https://ww5.komen.org/uploadedFiles/_Komen/Content/About_Us/Media_Center/Newsroom/breast-cancer-fact-sheet-august-2018.pdf